Opening the way

Practical
ideas for
all-age
worship

Tony Castle

Kevin Mayhew

First published in 2001 by
KEVIN MAYHEW LTD
Buxhall, Stowmarket, Suffolk IP14 3BW
Email: info@kevinmayhewltd.com

The hymns quoted can be found in both of the following: *Complete
Anglican Hymns Old and New* (Kevin Mayhew, 2000) and *Liturgical
Hymns Old and New* (Kevin Mayhew, 1999).

9 8 7 6 5 4 3 2 1 0

ISBN 1 84003 749 0
Catalogue No 1500439

Cover design by Jonathan Stroulger
Edited by Katherine Laidler
Typesetting by Louise Selfe
Printed in Great Britain

CONTENTS

For Tom
My dedicated assistant

The publishers wish to express their gratitude to the following for permission to include copyright material in this book:

Church House Publishing, Church House, Great Smith Street, London, SW1P 3NZ, for the extract *The Promise of His Glory* (page 5 of *The People's Book* – Introductory Outline) © The Central Board of Finance of the Church of England, 1990, 1991.

McCrimmon Publishing Co., 10-12 High Street, Great Wakering, Southend-on-Sea, Essex, SS3 0EQ, for the extract from *Fields of Praise* by John Harriott.

Oxford University Press, Great Clarendon Street, Oxford, OX2 6DP, for the extract from *Lark Rise* by Flora Thompson.

Every effort has been made to trace the owners of copyright material and we hope that no copyright has been infringed. Pardon is sought and apology made if the contrary be the case, and a correction will be made in any reprint of this book.

INTRODUCTION

The children I was accompanying on holiday were having a wonderful time, jigging up and down to the music and totally involved in the action songs. We were at a holiday centre and in the ballroom for the evening entertainment. Most popular with all age groups were the action songs, like *Music Man*, which involved the whole person: listening, singing and action. Along with many another adult, I was dragged to my feet by the children to take part; it was truly an all-age experience that engaged you completely and I have to admit, it was great fun. Everyone was on their feet; all united in the simple pleasure.

Released at last to return to the quiet of the sidelines and my seat, I reflected seriously upon the scene, human involvement and worship. The innocent fun that everyone was having: grandparents dancing with young grandchildren; fathers dancing with toddlers in their arms; mothers and daughters swinging round in time with one another. Harmony and unity, love and peace; there could be no doubt that Christ was present here, among his people. If only our Sunday worship, I pondered, had as much all-age and all-gender involvement; as much vitality, unity and peace.

The Church of England's *Common Worship* states that one of its aims is to encourage 'an imaginative engagement in worship, opening the way for people in the varied circumstances of their lives to experience the love of God in Jesus Christ in the life and power of the Holy Spirit'.

Not long ago I spent three weeks in Bangladesh, visiting relief and development programmes. On one occasion we were visiting a school for poor and disadvantaged children. It had little more than three simple rooms, with mud walls and floors and no glass in the windows. There were some rough old desks in two of the three rooms, but the smaller pupils, in class one, sat on the floor on rush matting. They were learning by rote.

At right angles to the single-storey, corrugated-iron-roofed school was another similar building. I stepped inside while waiting for the rest of the party to catch up – I'd wandered ahead – and saw another mud floor and more mud walls. At first I could see no decoration or suggestion of what it was used for, and then I noticed the tiniest of crucifixes hanging in the centre of the far wall, above a table. Then I saw, in the corner, on a wooden shelf, a very small simple statue of the Virgin Mary. It was a church! Shortly afterwards the children were brought in, with two young male teachers carrying a drum and a small hand-operated harmonium (seen all over

5

Bangladesh). The place was transformed! The music, the dance and the songs of the children, sang with gusto and joy – it was such an uplifting little service. I was reminded that it's the people who are the 'Church', not the building.

As we drove back to Mymensingh after we had reluctantly waved goodbye (the children are not accustomed to waving) I reflected that perhaps they, in that poor developing nation, have the balance right and we, the wealthy of the West, have it wrong. We have put much energy, money and resources into the church building (often nearly empty) and so little into building the real 'Church', God's people.

I hope that many more books, in the coming years, will assist in 'opening the way' for people to experience worship with more 'imaginative engagement' in the varied circumstances of their lives. This book is just one simple pastoral offering. At this time the three areas that appear to me to merit particular attention – with a few ideas and suggestions – are

- the Christian year, which is our liturgical framework
- the hymns we sing, which are so often chosen for the wrong reasons
- education together in the Christian faith, for so many strange concepts are still around

If some of these practical suggestions prove to be helpful in stimulating the reader to 'open the way' to her or his own imaginative engagement, it will have achieved its purpose.

Tony Castle

SECTION ONE
Celebrating the Christian Year

PART ONE
The Christian Year

It is a puzzle to many children and young people that we celebrate the birth of Jesus and then less than four months later we are talking about his death on the cross. While the Christian year helps us to enter more deeply into the mystery of Christ's life, death and resurrection, it is not helpful to suggest that the year is tied to or follows the order of his life, which it clearly does not.

It is more understandable for ordinary people if we approach the mystery of Christ through his twin commandments: 'Love God' and 'Love your neighbour'. The simplest and most helpful description of God in the New Testament is in the first letter of John: 'God is love' (4:16). It is from our appreciation of God's love for us, and our developing love for him, that our faith, hope and love are nourished.

One way to understand and use the Christian year is to see it in terms of love, inspired by the simple phrase 'Love came down at Christmas', prompted by the text, 'God so loved the world that he gave his Son' (John 3:16):

- The *Coming* of Love – Advent
- The *Showing* of Love – Christmas and Epiphany
- The *Offering* of Love – Lent and Holy Week
- The *Triumph* of Love – Easter
- The *Giving* of Love – Time after Pentecost

Advent *The Coming of Love*

This preparation period of the Christian year, called the 'Coming', is well named, for Advent covers not one but three 'Comings' of Christ:

- The Coming of Love as a baby – the first Coming of Jesus as a member of the human family
- The Coming of Love as a preacher – the second Coming of Jesus at the age of 30 as a rabbi
- The Coming of Love as the judge – the final Coming of Christ at the end of time as our judge and king

In the four weeks of Advent these three Comings of Jesus are recalled. In worship where very young children are involved it might prove confusing if more than the first Coming is concentrated on. However, older children need not be confused if there is clear and careful explanation. Few older parishioners will have realised that Advent has these three threads to it, and their observance of the season might be freshened and become more satisfying with the realisation.

Just as in ordinary family life, so in the family life of the community much is learnt in an accumulative way, by constant repetition. The Christian year, like the seasons, comes round and round again. We do not need to be anxious about doing, learning and understanding everything at once.

Christmas and Epiphany

The Showing of Love

The birth of a first baby is an exciting time in a family. With understandable pride the parents show off the sign of their love for one another to family, friends and neighbours. Church communities should try never to miss the opportunity to be part of this loving celebration. For example, it is so much more convenient and tidy to have the baptism or the dedication of a baby as a private family service, but the extra work and trouble taken to involve the community, at a public Sunday service, has an incalculable benefit and value for all. The genuine joy and expressions of love and support from everyone around the couple make the occasion unique in all human experience.

Christmas is surely the most popular of the Christian festivals because deep down, beneath all the commercialism, it is the celebration of such a love. At the divine level, God shows his love by the gift of his Son. At the human level a young couple, Mary and Joseph, have a first baby and, having no family close by, show the child off, first to the shepherds and later to the Magi.

Setting aside here any questions of literary criticism, Luke and Matthew, in their quite different versions of the nativity story, point to the future Messiah as the Good Shepherd, as well as Lord of all nations and King of kings.

Christmas is a birthday celebration, not of a dead hero but of a living Lord. There would be no Christmas festival, for anyone, if there were no triumphant resurrection. It is the risen Lord we celebrate with at Christmas. The festival is less about an historical event (so it is not important that we do not know the actual day or even the year that Christ was born) and more about celebrating Christ's continuing presence with us.

Lent and Holy Week   *The Offering of Love*

'Canoe leader risks life to keep group together'
'Wife throws herself in front of husband as terrorist fires'
'Scout leader shields Scout's body with his own, in rock avalanche'

From time to time our daily newspapers carry stories of heroic self-sacrifice, when the natural impulse for self-preservation is courageously set aside. Such generous action does not come naturally, for all humans are born with a necessary strong self-love. With the passing of the years this has to be broadened out, channelled and developed, so that while retaining a healthy self-love (to take proper care of oneself) in-growing love is turned out to include others.

The learning goes on all through life, the really mature person being the one who is the most unselfish, with the greatest love and consideration for others. Jesus summed it up when he said, 'Greater love has no one than this, that he lay down his life for his friends' (John 15:13).`

For most Christians the effort to live unselfishly is a daily struggle. Self-discipline is called for, and Lent is the season which encourages us to concentrate on this in preparation for Easter, the celebration of Christ's heroic self-sacrifice.

So Lent is

- a time for a change of heart, for a closer look at the way our lives are lived

- a time for concern for others, caring by personal action or gifts to charity

- a time for prayer that costs, in terms of time and effort

All three strike at personal selfishness and the roots of sin. A closer look at our lives will reveal areas that need dealing with. Concern for others encourages us to put others before our own self-interest, and an effort to set time aside for prayer helps us to put God first and receive the help we need to live the Christian life. Only Easter, when the Lord offered himself for us, makes sense of Lent. We cannot spiritually go down into the grave with Christ on Good Friday and rise up to a new life with him on Easter Day, if we have not made some preparation beforehand. 'If we die with him, we will also live with him' (2 Timothy 2:11).

Easter   *The Triumph of Love*

The Israelites were so triumphant, after they had passed safely out of slavery in Egypt and through the Red Sea, that they burst

11

into song (Exodus 15:1-18): 'In your unfailing love you will lead the people you have redeemed' (verse 13).

That triumph of God's love has been celebrated by the Jewish people from that day to this, in the annual festival of Pesah or Passover. It recalls how blood shed and placed on the door-frame protected the people of Israel, when the firstborn of the Egyptians died; the final blow that persuaded Pharaoh to let the people go.

Was it just providential, or by the deliberate planning of Christ, that his arrest, death and resurrection took place at Pesah? Of all the days in the year none was more appropriate and significant. From the very earliest days of Christianity, even before Christ's followers were called 'Christians', the vital link and connection of the Lamb of God's sacrificial death and triumphant resurrection with the events of Exodus 11-20 was appreciated.

Once the individual Christian appreciates the significance of the triumph of God's love at the first Passover, in Egypt, and the triumph of God's love in the 'passover' of Christ, then the realisation dawns that the 'resurrection theme' is at the very centre of each individual's life. And each and every day of that life.

It is not just the seasons of the year that see the death and rebirth of nature; nor each day that dies at dusk and rises afresh with the sun. Daily, each person is tempted, falls, and rises to follow the Son of God anew.

How many times in every normal person's life is there a losing and a finding; a crisis and a recovery; a loss of employment and a new opening; a breakdown in friendship and a new love; an illness and a restoration to good health; a death in the family and a birth? And, for the faithful Christian, all things work together for good and for the final triumph of love.

Pentecost   *The Giving of Love*

In secondary education these days, pupils are encouraged to learn at least two foreign languages. They will also learn other languages. There is, for example, computer language; there is body language; and when young people start to drive they will have to master the language of the Highway Code.

According to Genesis, God intended that the unity of the human race should be assured through the use of one language. Human pride brought confusion, as the Tower of Babel story explains (Genesis 11:1-9), and when 'the Lord confused the language of the whole world', disunity reigned.

Lovers speak the same language, in more than one sense, and often have their own language – as the romantic entries

12

in national newspapers reveal on St Valentine's Day. Love shares knowledge. God so loved the world that he spoke his word – all the knowledge that he encompasses – in human terms (Christmas). The Word of God, or the Son, so loved God the Father that he gave total obedience and the sacrifice of his whole self (Easter).

Because of his nature, which is love – 'God is love', John tells us in 1 John 4:16 – God is compelled to communicate. This he does, as we do, through signs. The Feast of Pentecost is rich in God's sign language. 'Suddenly a sound like the blowing of a violent wind came from heaven and filled the whole house . . . they saw what seemed to be tongues of fire that separated and came to rest on each of them' (Acts 2:2-3). Wind – the breath of God – and fire symbolised not just God's presence, but also his love.

The fire of God's love enters the lives of the Apostles and they are transformed. The 'tongues' of Pentecost heal and unite, where the 'tongues' of Babel had sown division and disunity.

The language of love is a gift; lovers always want to give to one another. In the parable of the last judgement in Matthew 25:31-46, the story of the separation of the sheep from the goats, it is those who are the givers who are rewarded, while the takers are banished to eternal punishment. The message is that eternal life is for those who have shown their love for Christ, by giving their time and their energy to caring for their neighbours. This follows, of course, the model given them by Christ at the Last Supper (John 13:1-16) when he rises from the table to wash the feet of his friends. Such love is the gift of the Spirit of Love bestowed at Pentecost.

Time after Pentecost   *The Living of Love*

It is one thing to receive a gift, quite another to appreciate and use it. The gift of God's love is offered to all and particularly to those who, following Christ, have shown some desire to live by his way. Indeed, those first followers who lived by the gift of the Spirit were called 'the people of the way' (Acts 9:2 and 24:14). However, only a small number respond to the gift and that response varies from person to person.

The Parable of the Sower comes to mind, where the seed is the gift of God's Spirit of Love. Some seed fell along the path, where it was trampled on. Some fell on rock, where it withered away. Some fell among thorns and was choked by them. And some fell on good soil, yielding a crop. The gift, offered to all, is the same; the response is individual. God respects every person's freedom; he never forces anyone.

The traditional colour used for church vestments at this time of the year is green, the colour of growing plants, grass and greenery. The growth looked for is not in church attendance or 'churchy' activities, but in personal spiritual development, in Gospel values and in the yield of a good crop.

Living a life of love, in a family setting, is one of constant service. It is often an uphill struggle to respond generously. There is the endless round of chores and duties to be fulfilled: clearing up after children, sorting out their squabbles, keeping up with the boring round of washing, ironing, cooking. No other way of life offers so much aggravation and temptation to quit, nor such an opportunity to grow in patience, love and maturity. In a word, in *holiness*. The living love in the family is the God-given way for most Christians to grow.

Much the same can be said of those who care for someone with a physical or mental disability, an ageing and bedridden relative, or terminally-ill patient. It is a living-out of the Easter theme, of dying to oneself in the service of others.

Jesus got up from the supper table (John 13:4ff) and put an apron round him and then knelt before each of his friends and washed their feet. Then he said, 'I have set you an example to do as I have done for you.' Clearly the badge of the true Christian is the apron, the apron of the Suffering Servant.

Practical pointers The loneliness of the person who lives alone can be crucifying too, especially in our society where the media extol couples and there is a very real fear of going out after dark. The local church family needs to be aware of such people and help them too to grow by drawing them into an 'apron' Christianity. (Growth does not stop because people are old or housebound.) There are always interests and tasks available to such members of the community, if there is a willingness to serve, though their willingness may need nurturing by confidence-building. The tasks can be as simple as folding the weekly newsletters, making tea or coffee for the harassed helpers at the church mother and toddler group, or reading to the children of such a group. It could be baby-sitting so that a young couple can go out and have a little time to themselves; sitting with a bedridden church member; helping with Christian Aid coffee morning, and so on. If practical action is difficult, there is still the valuable work of prayer. Our daily papers and the community's sick list will provide plenty of reasons to pray.

The work of the Spirit is growth in unity, love, joy and peace. The church community grows through mutual service and support, and everyone, of whatever age or situation, can follow the example of Christ the servant, if they appreciate and use the gifts of the Holy Spirit.

A note on charismatic gifts

All Christians receive charismatic gifts, and all Christians are charismatic. For 'no one can say, Jesus is Lord, except by the Holy Spirit' (1 Corinthians 12:3). No genuine gift of the Holy Spirit will ever divide or estrange others, nor will it breed pride, for that is the way of Babel, not the way of Pentecost.

Charismatic gifts are not for the individual and personal use of a Christian. Christianity is a community faith, as we saw earlier, so the gifts of the Spirit are for the upbuilding of the Christian as a member of the community. Each gift is for sharing and for the development of the community. 'The manifestation of the Spirit is for the common good' (1 Corinthians 12:31).

Harvest

In the largely urban life of the modern Christian, the link with the soil and the gathering-in of the harvest has become tenuous. Most of us are more familiar with stacks of canned food, often from the tropics. Yet Harvest Festival can still play an important liturgical role, not only in expressing gratitude to our Creator Father for all his goodness and care of us, but also as a celebration of the gathering-in of a spiritual harvest, along the lines that we have been exploring.

All Saints

The festival of All Saints, which ends the Christian year, is easily linked with the harvest of the fruits of the Spirit in those members of our local community whose lives have been an admirable example.

All Saints' tide provides the opportunity to turn away from the ordinary time of the Church Year in an autumn month that has its own secular echoes of death and remembering. Sanctity is – in spite of everything – accessible to people, not as a nice idea but as a reality pumped into the bloodstream of the human race by God's action in the lives of his saints. The dark side of that confident rejoicing in our fellowship with the saints is the Church mourning her departed and commending them in faith and trust to God. This commemoration is a proper corrective to the rather forced jollity which is sometimes substituted for a sober confidence in the power of God alone to bring life out of death, light out of darkness. While we rejoice in the heroic example of the saints, we feel the loss of those we know and love, and many people are helped by holding together these two commemorations.

The Promise of His Glory

PART TWO
Ideas for All-age Services
Based on the Christian Year

This section offers guidelines for complete all-age events based on the Christian year. Teams who are exploring all-age worship for the first time may find them useful guides. Others may find some ideas, insights or readings to add to their own rich store of experience.

Advent

Background note The word 'Advent' is derived from the Latin for 'coming' or 'arrival'. The season was developed in the Western Church as a preparation for the Nativity, in imitation of Lent, which is much earlier in origin. Church councils held in Gaul in the sixth century refer to Advent as a period of six weeks before Christmas, with fasting on each Monday, Wednesday and Friday. In other countries, five weeks was the norm. However, by the eighth century, throughout Europe, Advent had become a four-week season.

Biblical note From a biblical perspective the words 'coming' and 'Messiah' are interconnected. The expected coming of the Messiah is what is celebrated throughout Advent and Christmas. Through the dark days of the Exile in Babylon and the oppression of Greek and Roman occupation, the Jewish People longed for a 'Son of David' to come. So Isaiah could prophesy: 'The people walking in darkness have seen a great light; on those living in the land of the shadow of death a light has dawned' (Isaiah 9:2).

Visual/decoration Advent is a time of preparation for the joy and excitement of Christmas, a quiet 'low' period before the 'high' of the festive season. So it is traditional not to have flower arrangements during Advent. In fact, it is an ideal time to get a working party together to give the church a thorough clean and tidy up. The stark simplicity of Advent is an important reminder of its role.

Advent wreaths have become widely used in recent years. Many churches place a large evergreen wreath, with four red or purple candles (some add a white one in the centre, as a Christmas candle) on a special stand or table clearly in view near the altar. During the introductory rites a child or young person is invited to come forward and light the candle for that Sunday.

Jesse Tree An ancient practice which is becoming popular again is the Jesse Tree, a custom dating from the Middle Ages. A branch of a large bush or a small tree is stripped of its leaves, painted silver, and is set in a bucket of sand (or one of those Christmas tree holders that you can buy from a garden centre). On the branches the children hang cut-out figures representing people and events in the Old Testament that prepared the way for the coming of Jesus. For example, creation can be symbolised by a cut-out sun and moon, the fall of Adam and Eve by an apple, Noah and family by a cardboard ark, Isaac by a bundle of sticks, Jacob by a ladder, King David by a harp, and so on. This too can be added to before the weekly Sunday service, before or after the lighting of the next Advent candle.

If you are interested in pursuing the idea of the Jesse Tree, I recommend that you acquire a copy of *The Jesse Tree: an Advent Activity Book* by Katie Thompson (published by Kevin Mayhew). Katie says, 'The Jesse Tree provides a fun way to trace the "royal roots" of Jesus, by discovering Christ's "family tree".' The book is immensely practical and the author really makes the whole enterprise fun.

Exploring the theme The key features of Advent are the coming of the Messiah and the kingdom that he preached; the watching and the waiting; the expectant longing, in a spirit of penitence, for the fulfilment of the promise made to the people of the old covenant.

Modern Christians, affected by non-Christian popular culture, may start celebrating the Nativity, with Christmas trees and decorations long before 25 December. But in the Church year the celebrating begins on Christmas Day and extends to 6 January.

Music Christmas carols have little place in Advent – how can we seriously be *coming* and at the same time be celebrating *an arrival.* Ideally – and for most it will remain an ideal – we should try to avoid the popular pressure (and misunderstanding) to use them. Perhaps the most we will be able to do is keep them for the latter part of Advent. An explanation is sometimes called for. Putting it simply, you cannot expectantly and excitedly wait for the arrival of something (or someone) and simultaneously sing in celebration of its arrival!

Advent music should be chosen to reflect the theme. The following are suitable choices:

- Come, thou long-expected Jesus
- Hark! A herald voice is calling
- How lovely on the mountains
- O come, O come, Emmanuel
- Wake up, O people

Readings The emphasis in the Lectionary readings for the first two Sundays of Advent is on the coming of Christ as judge. Later there is a shift to his coming as a child, and, as a plan to cover all three 'comings' in one Advent service (are not three necessary?), the following outline could be used:

- 'Your God is coming' (Isaiah 35:1-6, 10) – *the coming of the Messiah as a preacher*
- 'Be patient' (James 5:7-10) – *his coming as Judge*
- 'She will give birth to a son' (Matthew 1:18-25) – *the coming of the Incarnate Word*

Introduction

Four volunteers are needed to stand before the people in a line to take the parts below (or similar ones). In addition, four children (two for each poster) hold two five-foot lengths of wallpaper with the words 'Coming' and 'Hope' clearly printed on the blank side. These can be held on either side of the four volunteers so that people can see them clearly.

The four speakers say:

- '**I am an expectant mother**. The birth of my baby is coming . . . I hope for a healthy baby.'
- '**I am a schoolboy (girl)**. The Christmas holidays are coming . . . I hope for lots of Christmas presents.'
- '**I am a pensioner**. My family are coming to see me at Christmas . . . I hope to find them all well and happy.'
- '**I am a driver/florist/secretary** (*or whatever*). My retirement is coming soon . . . I am hoping for time to expand my interests.'

The leader then says: 'The keywords from each of our friends' statements are *coming* and *hope*, and these are the keywords for the whole of Advent, and our service today.'

The service proceeds with the opening hymn or call to worship.

Children's address

The leader hides a box of sweets near to where he or she is to speak. A large card, nicely decorated and with the word 'Christmas' clearly printed on it, needs to be propped up in a position where the leader can walk past it and have space before and after the card. The children's address can go along these lines:

'In a few minutes I am going to invite all you children to come up here and I will give you something. Now, suddenly, you are very interested; you are hoping for something good; there is an air of expectancy. You are beginning to think: how long before he will give us this surprise gift; how long have we got to wait?

'That is what it was like for the Jewish people before the

birth of Jesus, the Messiah. They believed that God would send them a good leader. They were waiting in hope; nothing happened for a long time, but they kept waiting and hoping for God's gift to them. *(Leader walks to the far side of the place where the large card has been placed.)* In front of me is the word "Christmas". It's like that now. Christmas lies ahead of us; it has not yet arrived – just a few more weeks to go. If I walk slowly towards this word "Christmas", that is like the passing of time. Now I have arrived at the card and, before I know it, I'm past. Christmas is behind me. Now I have to look back to it.

'That is what happens every year. Christmas seems a long time coming and then it is here, and then gone. (You are still waiting and hoping for what I have hidden for you.) The Jewish people waited for a long time for Jesus to be born, as the Christ; and because he was not quite what they expected, many of them did not accept God's gift.

'You are all anxious to know what it is that I have for you; you must wait patiently. That is what the Jewish people had to do as they waited for the Messiah to be born; they had to be patient.

'That is the lesson of Advent; we have to learn *patience*. God will always answer our prayers, but not necessarily in the way we expect, and sometimes he makes us wait quite a long time for an answer. But it will come. *(Leader returns to starting point and produces the box of sweets.)*

'Now the time has come. Come up two or three at a time and help yourselves to a sweet.'

Advent wreath   After the Gospel reading, the first (or next) candle may be lit. (See *The Promise of His Glory*, pp. 137-39, for an accompanying prayer.)

Adults' address   Three of the previous four volunteers are needed again: the expectant mother, the schoolchild and the pensioner. (Take care to balance the genders.) They are asked to stand near the leader, in full view. The card used for the children's address is replaced with one which has the words: 'Baby', 'Teacher', 'Judge'. The leader says:

'We have already learnt that the season of Advent is about the words *coming* and *hope*. You heard how the children were told that another important word is *patience*. How do these three words link with our three volunteers standing here, and with Advent itself? Let's all go and stand beside the card which has the words 'Baby', 'Teacher' and 'Judge'. *(Group stands to left of the card, as seen by the congregation.)*

'There are three Comings of Christ – as baby, as teacher and, in the future, as judge. Our expectant mother here is waiting patiently for the coming of her baby, and with her we all hope it will be strong and healthy when it is born. *(The woman crosses to the other side of the card.)* Jesus has already come as a baby.

'When we see our schoolgirl (boy) standing here, we see the uniform and we are reminded of our local school and its teachers. *[Name of child]* has to work and study patiently at school and hopes that the teachers will give him/her a proper, balanced education. *(Child crosses to other side of the card.)* Jesus has already come as a teacher.

'Our pensioner here is grateful for the many life experiences he/she has had and is aware of successes and failures in the past. Aware, too, that at some point in the future Christ will pass a judgement on them. But that has not yet come; Christ has still to come as judge for each one of us. *(Speaker returns to original point, leaving the expectant mother and child on the right of the card and the pensioner still standing on the left.)*

'The season of Advent is given to us to remember and think about these three comings of Christ. So the readings of Advent speak of John the Baptist, who prepared the people for the arrival of Jesus as a teacher; and there are readings too to remind us that Christ will judge each of us, at the end of our own lives and at the end of the world. So Advent is not just about preparing for the birth of the special baby on 25 December as the Advent calendars would have us believe.'

Intercessions   These can be led by the four volunteers.

(Expectant mother)
Caring Creator and Father,
you have made all things
and care for the tiniest of your creatures.
As we prepare for the birthday of your Son
as a tiny child,
we ask your blessing on all women
who, at this time, are expecting a child,
the work of your creation.

Prepare us, O Lord:
Make us ready for Christ's coming.

(Schoolchild)
Father of all knowledge and wisdom,
you desire all people to grow in understanding
and develop to their fullest potential.

21

As we prepare for the birthday of your Son
who became the world's greatest and most important teacher,
we ask your blessing on all who teach
and learn in our schools.

Prepare us, O Lord:
Make us ready for Christ's coming.

(Pensioner)
Ageless God and Father,
you live a timeless existence
and never grow old.
As we prepare for the birthday of your Son
who shared all the joys and anxieties that we experience,
we ask your blessing on those who are worried
about ageing, living alone and their health.

Prepare us, O Lord:
Make us ready for Christ's coming.

(Other intercessory prayers may be added, of course, as required.)

Parting scripts Reproduce the following twelve texts, cut them into individual little scripts and roll them tightly, so that each one comes out as a tiny scroll. Produce enough for every person at the service to have one, then pack them, mixed up, like little cylinders in two or three boxes. Arrange for two or three volunteers to stand at the church door as the people leave. Before the final blessing, the minister should encourage all to take a 'thought' for Advent as they leave.

Let us live
faithfully, justly, peacefully
in this world,
awaiting the blessed hope
and advent of the glory
of the great God.

Let what is crooked in me
become straight,
let what is rough become smooth,
and what is empty be filled.

We wait for your loving
kindness, O God,
to be revealed to us.

May God the Father,
who loved the world so much
that he gave his Son,
give you grace to prepare
for everlasting life.

O Lord of hosts, restore us;
if your face shine upon us,
then we shall be safe.

May God himself,
the God of everlasting peace,
make you perfect and holy
for the coming of his Son,
Jesus Christ.

The people who walked
in darkness
shall see a great light.

Lord Jesus, the prophets said
you would bring peace.
Give peace to our troubled hearts,
now and always.

Withhold your wrath
from us, O Lord,
and remember no more
our evildoing.

Lord Jesus,
John told the people to prepare,
for you were very near.
As Christmas approaches
help me to be ready
to welcome your coming.

Lord, let me hear the call
of your prophet, John,
that I may truly repent
and prepare.

When you come,
as judge, Lord Jesus,
may you find me
ready and prepared.

Christmas

Background note

It is at Rome in the early fourth century that we find the first evidence of Christmas being celebrated by the Christian community. In AD 274 the Emperor Aurelian introduced in the imperial capital the festival of the Invincible Sun (Natalis Solis Invicti) on 25 December. At some point before AD 336 (the first recorded date of Christmas) the Church, having no certain date of Christ's birth, must have taken this date to commemorate the Incarnation, the birth of the Sun of Righteousness.

Biblical note

The nativity stories occur in only two places in the New Testament, the first two chapters of both Matthew and Luke. These stories stand in isolation and arise from traditions different from those found elsewhere in the four Gospels. There are tensions between the two versions.

Modern Christians need to read reflectively what the text says, as distinct from what they think it says. For example, the visitors from the east are not 'kings' but 'Magi' or astrologers (Matthew 2:1). It does not say there were three visitors. It *does* say that three gifts were brought but three gifts can be brought by four people or ten people. They did not find a baby in a stable – the child was probably about eighteen months old (see verse 16) and the family was dwelling in a house ('on coming to the house' – verse 11).

Some of these discoveries may disturb some Christians, fearful that the challenge to their traditional understanding, perhaps from much earlier times, threatens the real meaning of Christmas. With explanation and mature thought they can be helped to see that the 'trappings' of the festival are of some value, but the real meaning lies beneath them.

The key text which sums up the message of Christmas is from John's Gospel: 'The Word became flesh and made his dwelling among us' (John 1:14). Essentially Christmas is not the celebration of a past historical event but of the wondrous belief that the Son of God became one of us and, as the risen Christ, is ever-present with us.

Visual/decoration

Most churches have their own customs, but it is good to question these from time to time, to bring freshness and to ensure that they are achieving their aim. Decoration can be for decoration's sake (good in itself), or it can be used to teach at the same time. This, of course, was the purpose of the old pre-Reformation wall paintings in parish churches.

Another challenge is to involve more than a small group in the work of decoration. It is possible to share out the windowsills and pillars among the church groups, not forgetting the children and young people. All-age decoration, in other words. The Guides, Scouts and Brownies can be allotted a portion of the church, along with the women's groups – and men's. The regular decorators can take care of the big Christmas tree or the crib, if there is one.

Crib decorators should be discouraged from putting the Wise Men in or near the crib. According to Matthew's Gospel these figures did not arrive at Christmas but some time later. These figures should only be added on the Epiphany, 6 January. This will give an added focus for that great festival, which is otherwise easily overshadowed. A visual idea for the Epiphany is given later.

The decorating working parties would find it helpful and encouraging if they are given themes for their designs – for example, Light of the World, Holy Family, Prince of Peace, Dwelt among us, Glory to God.

Introduction   As soon as all are gathered, before the commencement of the service proper, the minister stands before the congregation with a basket of fresh holly leaves (already stripped from the branch). He or she invites two people from each bench, or each family – the youngest and the eldest – to come forward. As they approach, the minister places a holly leaf carefully in the open palm of the hand, with the words, 'Keep a generous open hand, like God.' They return to their places. The minister addresses the people, along these lines:

'This is a joyous day, a happy occasion, but it is not without its reminder of the painful side of life. The Christians of the Middle Ages appreciated that the birth of the Son of God was not without pain and inconvenience. They used the holly bush, with its evergreen leaves and prickly thorns, as a symbol. The evergreen reminds us of the ever-present risen Christ who helps us to grow as Christians. The sharp prickles remind us of the crown of thorns of Jesus, placed upon his head before he died for us. They also remind us that our lives have "prickly" parts to them.

'The holly leaves were given out with the words, "Keep a generous open hand, like God", to remind us today of God's openhanded generosity – he so loved the world that he gave his Son. If you close your hand, if you are tight-fisted with others, there will be pain, not happiness.

'Now sing together the carol "The holly and the ivy".' *(This can be the opening hymn of the service.)*

Exploring the theme

The Christmas celebration is about the wondrous mystery of the Incarnation. It is not so much the birth of the historical Jesus that we seek to recall, but the meaning for us now of the Word made flesh and the presence with us of the Risen Christ. It is possible for modern Christians to be content with looking back two thousand years to a baby in a manger and to fail to understand the deeper significance of the festival.

Music

This is not the time for new hymns and experimentation. There will be people in the congregation who do not attend regularly and they should not feel excluded by the choice of music. Many carols, ancient and modern, are popular and suitable.

Readings

These are well known and prescribed by tradition. If this service is taking the place of a family service on Christmas morning, then any reading(s) preceding the following dramatic presentation should be kept very short. Select four 'actors' to take the parts, rehearse and, if possible, provide them with costumes.

Before the service begins they are in the church, welcoming the congregation (answering no questions about their role in the service) and giving out hymn books.

Before the Gospel reading (Luke 2:4-16) the actors come to the front and face the congregation to present 'The no-good shepherd boy' (see page 27). The reading then follows.

The no-good shepherd boy

Scene:	In a market area of Jerusalem, near the Sheep Gate
Time:	Early evening on 24 December, 6 BC
Present:	• A scruffy-looking shepherd, a young lad • A richly adorned woman, middle-aged • A priest, elderly • A modestly dressed woman, elderly

Shepherd I've come into the city to buy some food for our group; it's likely to be cold out in the fields tonight. We spend all our time with the sheep. We can't get to the synagogue on the Sabbath. Everyone else looks down on us because we can't keep all the laws, especially the purity laws.

Rich woman I'm the wife of a very wealthy Sadducee. My husband owns several shops and has a prosperous trading company. Of course, he attends the local synagogue and we bought it a new scroll only last week. What is this scruffy shepherd doing here?

Priest I am one of the chief priests. I've just come from working in the Temple all day – we offered thirty-seven sacrifices today. The Temple is my life. I keep every one of the Jewish laws and I know God is pleased with me. What is that scruffy, irreligious shepherd doing here? It's about time they were banned from coming into the Holy City.

Elderly woman My husband is the oldest serving member of the Sanhedrin, the council. He's a highly respected rabbi and Pharisee, well known for the long religious fasts he keeps. We have a lovely country house out at Bethlehem and an apartment here in the city. My husband would soon send this filthy shepherd boy packing.

Shepherd   [*aside to congregation*] You see, these respectable folk have no time for the likes of me.

Rich woman   Excuse me, but I must be off. My husband and I are invited to a smart party at the High Priest's house this evening.

Priest   I beg your pardon, but I must go too. The priests have a meeting this evening to discuss the new rota of services at the Temple.

Elderly woman   Excuse me, but I must hurry home. My husband expects me home for the evening family prayers at dusk.

Shepherd   You see how nice respectable people look down on us shepherds. No parties for us; nothing exciting ever happens in our lives, it's so boring looking after sheep.

Music The carol 'While shepherds watch' can be sung immediately before or after the Gospel reading.

If the church has an orchestral group some light pieces can be played softly in the background during the readings. If there is no such group, Christmas is a fine opportunity to get together a few young flautists, guitarists and any other instrumentalists you may have in your church, to provide a simple background or accompaniment. (There is no need to be too adventurous to begin with.)

Address Today's theme is the dignity of the individual human person, arising from the belief that God's Son, the Word, became a human being. The Son of God became man so that humankind could become children of God. The divine seal was placed upon human dignity the moment the Word was born in the stable.

Did you get the point of 'The no-good shepherd boy'? Bethlehem is within easy walking distance of Jerusalem, and at the time of Christ's birth there were many very religious people and many wealthy people. There was the High Priest and members of his council, the rich merchants of the Sadducee families and members of the supreme council, the Sanhedrin. But not one of those was invited to the birth of the Messiah. When the long-awaited historic moment arrived – the birth of the promised Messiah – no religious or community leader was invited. No one from the rich and politically powerful families was invited. God only invited the looked-down-on and poor, marginalised shepherds. What a message for us!

Where would Christ be born today? Perhaps it would be among the homeless on London's streets, those lying in the doorway of Boots, along the Strand. Would the angel call at Buckingham Palace and leave an invitation to the birth there, or at Lambeth Palace for the Archbishop of Canterbury, or the Cardinal Archbishop of Westminster? According to Luke's Gospel, no. Who are the modern equivalent to the shepherds? Who do we – respectable, religious and fairly well-off – look down on?

God so loved the world – the poor, the disabled, the illiterate – that he gave his Son. Christmas is about human dignity. God does not judge people by what they possess, or the education they have received, or their career prospects. He does not 'see' colour or age or sex; God sees the loving heart. On this gift-giving day make a gift to God before you leave this church today – the genuine gift of your heart. Let us now sing the first and last verses of 'In the bleak mid-winter'. Apply the symbolism of the first verse not to the weather, but to the bleak materialistic world in which we live, where so many people's hearts are closed to those in need, where people are prejudiced against others, and are as 'hard as iron' in their business dealings.

Epiphany _____

Background note

The word Epiphany comes from the Greek for 'manifestation' or 'showing off'. The feast day has a long and complex history. At first, in the Eastern Church from the third century, 'the manifestation' referred to the revelation of God to the world in Jesus Christ. By the fourth century it was commemorating the birth of Jesus and his baptism. When the Western Church established 25 December as the festival of the Lord's birth, 6 January became the manifestation of the Child Jesus to the Magi. It is still kept as the festival of the Lord's baptism in the Eastern Church.

Biblical note

The Scripture text (Matthew 2:1-18) is overlaid with tradition. In the planning meeting it would be advisable to read the text and discuss it together. The focus is really on the gifts, not the visitors. It is the symbolism of the gifts which is important, pointing to the type of Messiah Jesus will be, not the number of the visitors or their traditional names. Matthew is keen to convince his Jewish readers that this very special child really does fulfil the Old Testament prophecies; he really has the credentials of the Messiah.

Visual/decoration

The symbolism of the three gifts is important and rather than emphasise the gift-bringers (the Magi), who have their own symbolic purpose, the decoration can focus on the gold, incense and myrrh. However, if the church has a public Christmas crib, the figures of the Magi can 'journey' to the stable, beginning the first Sunday after Christmas. They can start just inside the church, preferably on a table or some raised area, and can be moved every day to arrive on 6 January, then be placed in the crib at the start of that day's service.

There could be three flower arrangements, one for each gift, with the symbolism of each explored – regal colours with a touch of the oriental; for the incense, blue and silver; and for the myrrh, purple and magenta. Or one large arrangement could include all these colours.

Exploring the theme

The visitors to the child Jesus were not Jews, yet their story is only recorded in the Gospel written by a Jewish Christian for Jewish readers. So the 'showing' of Christ to the Gentiles must be significant. The gifts relate to the future role of the child as Messiah. For the Gentiles (and the Jews) he will be a king (gold), a priest (frankincense), and a suffering servant (myrrh), just as the prophets had foretold.

Music   Suitable music could include the following:
- As with gladness men of old
- Let all the world in every corner sing
- We three kings

Readings
- Isaiah 49:1-6: 'I will make you a light to the Gentiles.' The young girl who led in the ministers (see below) stands beside (a little behind) the reader during this reading. *Or* Isaiah 60:1-6: 'Nations will come to your light, and kings to the brightness of your dawn.' If there has been the opportunity to work with the children, these words (or the previous text) can appear on a decorated card and be held up beside the star.
- Ephesians 3:1-12 or 3:2-3a, 5-6: 'The Gentiles are heirs together with Israel, members together of one body, sharers in the promise of Christ Jesus.'
- Matthew 2:1-12: This reading is ideally suited for either a dramatised reading in parts, or acting out with actors' own parts and words, but well prepared and rehearsed. (See *The Dramatised Bible.*) It is vital that the wise 'men' are not all male, and there can be five or six visitors; this can be explained in the sermon.

Introduction   The choir and the ministers could be led in by a young girl (not vested) who carries a large silver star on a stick or pole. (The star can be simply made of card, covered with kitchen foil, mounted on a spare broom handle.)

   If appropriate, when all are gathered, the Magi crib figures can be ceremonially placed in the crib by people of different ages. The figures could be brought in as part of the entry procession, led by the star-bearer and to the accompaniment of the hymn, 'We three kings'.

Children's address   The star-bearer comes to stand beside the speaker. A boy goes to the crib and brings the 'baby', then stands beside the bearer of the star. The address is along these lines:

   'Did anyone here get a bike for Christmas? Did you go out and ride it on Christmas Day? Did you show it to your friends? When we have a lovely gift, we like to show it to our friends. We want other people to see and admire it.

'You see our star, here. The star showed the Magi (Wise Men) where the baby Jesus was. When the Magi arrived at the house where Mary and Joseph were (they had moved out of the stable by then) Mary showed Jesus to the visitors from the East. That is why this day is called the "Epiphany", because the word means "the showing". Jesus was God's very special gift. Although he was born a Jewish baby, he was not just for the Jewish people, but for all of us. We are what the Jews call "Gentiles". The baby here *(indicating the figure held alongside)* was shown to the Wise Men, who were the first Gentiles to be shown the baby. Those visitors stood for us.'

Adults' address The star-bearer and the baby-carrier stay within easy reach of the place where the sermon will be preached. Three elderly members of the congregation (if possible those who took parts in the Gospel dramatisation) go to the back of the church and collect the three gifts already prepared and left there: a box wrapped in gold paper; a censer or thurible with burning incense; and a small ornate, Eastern-looking jar or vase. The star-bearer walks to the back of the church to lead the three with the gifts forward. (There is no need for the 'Magi' to be dressed up.) The baby-carrier comes to the front step, into the sanctuary, and with the minister on his right stands facing the congregation and the advancing procession.

The adult address begins before the procession moves from the rear:

'Gifts usually express the sentiments "I love you" or "Thank you". These gifts which now approach say neither; they are prophetic gifts. That means that they look to the future, to the roles which this very special baby will fulfil.

'There is the gift of gold, for this baby will be a king. Remember the words of Pontius Pilate at Christ's final trial: "You are a king, then" (John 18:37). He is Christ, our king, who expects our loyalty and devotion.

'There is the gift of incense, associated with temple worship and priesthood. This baby will be a priest, offering himself on the altar of the cross. "He sacrificed . . . once for all when he offered himself" (Hebrews 7:27). He is Christ, the glory of the Father.

'There is the gift of myrrh, a symbol of suffering and death. This baby is destined to suffer; he will be the Suffering Servant of God. "He was despised and rejected, a man of sorrows, and familiar with suffering" (Isaiah 53:3). He is Christ, our model in the service of others.'

Candlemas _____

Background note

This day, 2 February, is the natural climax of the forty days of the Christmas/Epiphany season. Luke, the evangelist, closes his collection of nativity stories with the presentation of the child Jesus in the Temple, the purification of Mary, and the meeting which took place between Mary and the child and the saintly Simeon. Because the day encompasses all three happenings, no other ancient Christian festival has changed its name so many times over the centuries.

This day was first kept about AD 350 by the Christians of Jerusalem. By 542 it had spread throughout Europe and was then known as 'the Meeting' (Hypapante), referring to the meeting of Simeon and the Virgin Mary. And a little time later it was called 'Candlemas', because candles were blessed and distributed at the Eucharist. This was to call to mind the words of Simeon: 'a light for revelation to the Gentiles'. In more modern times it has been understood as a feast of the Lord, marking the end of the Christmas/Epiphany period and looking ahead to the soon-to-be-celebrated sufferings and death of Jesus.

Biblical note

Luke – the Gentile writer – jams in three Jewish religious ceremonies between verses 21 and 24 of chapter 2 of his Gospel: the naming of Jesus at his circumcision, the ritual purification of Mary after childbirth, as required by Leviticus 12, and the presentation of the infant Jesus, as the firstborn male child, to God, as required by Exodus 13:2.

Then follows the meeting between the child and Simeon, the righteous Jew, and his recognition of Jesus as the Messiah: 'the light for revelation to the Gentiles'. These words are closely followed by his words to Mary: 'a sword will pierce your own soul too'. This is the attraction of Candlemas today; not only does it mark the end of that circle of worship which began five weeks before, on the first Sunday of Advent, but it also points us on to Lent and Easter.

Visual/decoration

The two predominant liturgical colours today are white (to mark the link with the Christmas period) and purple (for the coming of the Lenten season). It is not a good time of the year for flowers, particularly purple ones, so other materials or fabrics can be used. A large display, close to the altar or beneath the pulpit, could use the three Epiphany figures, a large white candle, and two lengths of fabric, one white and one purple. Either drape the white (on the left as seen by the congregation) and the purple side by side over a raised mound and stand the candle in the centre; or drape the material round the foot of a large candlestick.

Place the three Magi figures round the candle, on the draped material, as in adoration of the candle (Christ, the Light of the World). Perhaps add a card with the message 'Christ, the Light of the World' or 'A light for revelation to the Gentiles'.

Exploring the theme There are several related themes to be found in this day's celebration. There is purification, presentation, meeting of the old and new covenants, Light of the World. Joy and sorrow are to be found; the joy of Simeon and Anna's greeting, but the sorrow in the words of Simeon's prophecy: 'a sword will pierce your own soul too'.

This day brings to an end the Christmas period, when the birth of Christ, the Light of the World, has been celebrated; the powers of darkness will triumph, briefly, in the coming season of the passion and death of Christ. The most appropriate theme then for our service is Christ, the Light of the World, 'the light for the revelation to the Gentiles'.

Music The music could include the following:
- Any version of 'Nunc Dimittis'
- Colours of day
- I watch the sunrise
- Lord, the light of your love (*Shine, Jesus, shine*)

Readings
- Exodus 12:51; 13:2, 11-16: 'Consecrate the first born to me.'
- Leviticus 12:6-8: The Law of Purification
- Isaiah 6:1-8: 'I saw the Lord fill the Temple.'
- Haggai 2:1-9: 'I will fill his house with splendour.'
- Luke 2:22-40: The Presentation

Introduction The traditional practice was to have a procession at the beginning of this service, which may or may not include the blessing of the candles carried by the congregation. It is most appropriate to gather everyone in a place separate from the church, perhaps in an adjoining hall. There the minister greets everyone and addresses them:

'Forty days ago we celebrated the joyful feast of the birth of Jesus our Lord. Today we recall the day on which he was presented in the Temple, fulfilling the law of Moses. We recall especially the prophetic words of Simeon: "a light for revelation to the Gentiles". To commemorate these words and those of Jesus himself later in his life – "I am the Light of The World" – we carry lighted candles into the church, while we sing the words of Simeon (Nunc Dimittis).'

The minister may now wish to bless the candles that the people are holding, with these or similar words:

Creator God, source of all light,
today you revealed to Simeon
your light of revelation to the nations.
Bless these candles;
may we who carry them praise your glory
and walk in the light of your love.
Amen.

The minister, carrying his own candle, leads the procession into the church.

The procession can wind its way around the church before the people file into their places. The candles are extinguished and the service then continues as usual.

Before the Gospel reading

The minister invites the oldest and the youngest person in each pew, or line of seats, to come out; only the older people bring their candles, which are lit when they reach the front of the church. (It would be as well to give warning of this before the service begins.) The child and the older person need not be from the same family or know one another. The 'couples' are invited to stand side by side, alternating old and young, close to where the Gospel is to be read. The minister introduces the reading with mention of the ancient name for this feast day, 'the Meeting' (see background note).

That is the meeting between the young Messiah, represented by the young people, and Simeon, represented by the older persons.

After the Gospel reading

The minister invites those representing Simeon to present their lighted candles to their younger companions. The minister then says (if appropriate):

At your baptism you were given a lighted candle like this, with the words: 'As Christ Jesus was a light to the nations, so must we give a shining example of really good, kind behaviour to others, so that they are drawn to be followers of Jesus, too.'

The candles are now extinguished and all return to their seats.

All-age address The minister goes and stands by the 'decoration' (see above) if there is one, or takes a large lighted candle in his hand, then says:

'Children always like candles. Is it the attraction of the unusual, the fascination with fire, the element of danger? Most of us never see a flame, like this one, lighting up a room. To us, with our bright fluorescent electric lights, a candle seems to give a very weak light. In the Science Museum in London they used to have a series of exhibits showing how light has been used, over the centuries, in homes. It started with the fires of the cavemen, the candles of the Middle Ages, through the oil lamps to the gas lights of the Victorians, and on to the modern electric lights brightly shining in all our homes. But when you sit in the dark, the lighting of a candle can bring you hope and joy.

'Imagine living in a country where for two whole months it never gets light. Every day it remains pitch black; there's not a glimmer of light to mark the difference between day and night. That is how it is for children of the town of Tromso in Norway, every year. Listen to this passage from a newspaper report:

> Somewhere behind the dark clouds, something stirred. One hundred and eighty brightly dressed children stared hopefully at the distant dark horizon.
>
> This was Tromsø, Norway – 215 miles inside the Arctic Circle and for the past two months in permanent darkness. Now, at eight minutes to midday, the sun was due back. Not for long, mind you – four minutes only on the first day. But it was enough to bring out a fair proportion of the 50,000 inhabitants of this, the world's most northerly city.
>
> The bells pealed out and hundreds of colourful balloons were sent flying high into the gloom. They had been looking forward to this moment since 25th November last, when the wan winter sun had finally sunk and day had become – night. For children, Sun Day – a celebration declared by King Olva in 1873 – means a day off school. One girl said, 'I'm so happy today. If you haven't lived through such a winter as ours, you can't imagine what it's like.'

'I couldn't, could you? Nor could anyone imagine what a difference the birth of Christ would make; how wonderfully he would be the light of the nations.

'Today is a special day because we can look back to the joy of Christmas (the white of our decoration) when the Light of the World was born; and forward (the purple) to the coming attempt by some to extinguish the Light by a brutal passion and death. As older people will know, life is made up of the white and the purple, and we need to keep our Christian light burning through both.'

Concluding note   If it is a eucharistic service any children who do not receive Communion could be invited to come up, to stand with candles alight around the altar (or suitable place) while Communion is distributed. The minister might like to explain this action in these or similar words:

'As we celebrate today the meeting of Simeon with the infant Messiah, it is fitting that our own "meeting" with Christ in this sacrament should be illuminated by the welcoming lights of our children.'

If desired, the children, holding their lighted candles, can wait to follow in the procession of ministers as it leaves the sanctuary.

Lent

Background note

The English word 'Lent', which means 'spring', does not express the significance of the six weeks of spiritual discipline in preparation for Easter. The fasting associated with Lent began with just six days (what we now know as Holy Week), but had been extended to five weeks by the time of the Council of Nicaea in AD 325. The longer period was primarily necessary because it had become a period of training and preparation for those who were to be baptised on Easter night. As fasting was never allowed on the Lord's Day (which celebrated the Resurrection), Sundays are not included in the forty days from Ash Wednesday to Easter.

Biblical note

Forty is the number traditionally associated with preparation, training and discipline. Jesus spent forty days and nights in the wilderness preparing for his ministry (Matthew 4:2). The Israelites were in the desert for forty years being shaped into God's people fit for the Promised Land (Exodus 16:35). Before God revealed himself to Elijah, the prophet had to travel for forty days and nights in which to fast and repent.

The ashes used by many to mark the commencement of the forty days is also very biblical; see the king of Nineveh (Jonah 3:6) and Job's repentance (Job 42:6). Jesus himself refers to the need for such signs of repentance (Matthew 11:21).

Visual/decoration

Lent is traditionally a time when the church remains undecorated with flowers, to fit the sombre nature of the season and to highlight the joy that follows. This does not exclude the use of other teaching visuals. The themes of repentance and 'making up' can be illustrated by the younger members of the church community and exhibited. There is a wonderful poster by Sieger Koder (available from St Paul Multimedia) on the reunion of the father and son, from the Prodigal Son. Also, excellent poster sets are available from Turvey Abbey. (Contact details are given on page 111.)

Exploring the theme

Several themes are interwoven in Lent. There is preparation for the central mystery of our faith; coping with temptation; conflict; suffering; repentance and renewal. It is an opportunity to face reality and the truth about oneself, to critically examine one's life and see if God's will is truly being sought and followed.

We shall prepare well for Easter if, like Jesus, we seek to do God's will, for to do that we have to face the truth and the conflict involved, which lead to a need for reconciliation and a fresh start.

In the Jewish tradition the story of Jonah is used at times of repentance and making a fresh start. Jesus himself made a link between the story of Jonah and the Easter event (Matthew 12:38-42). In this service we shall follow that example.

Music

Any music and hymns of a penitential nature are suitable, such as the following:

- Amazing grace
- Forty days and forty nights
- Do not be afraid
- God forgave my sin

Readings

As well as the readings given in the Lectionary for each Sunday of Lent, the following are also suitable:

- First reading: Jonah 1 and 2.
- Second reading: Matthew 12:38-42.

Introduction

Preparations for this service depend on how much trouble the planning team want to go to; there can be a simple or a more involved version. For the simple service, choose a cross-section of the congregation to take parts in the reading.

The more involved and more satisfying version would be to act out the reading, with props. A group of the young people can be invited to build a boat using cardboard boxes and other materials on one side of the sanctuary and paint the outline of a big fish on a large sheet of card, behind which 'Jonah' can duck, with his voice only heard. One of the church's youth groups might get involved in this as a Lenten project in the week prior to the service. Of course, the actors will have to be rehearsed.

Introductory address

So that all present will see the point of the play or part-reading which will take place at the usual time for the first reading, the minister needs to spend just a few minutes, either before the entry or first hymn, or immediately afterwards, explaining the Lenten themes to be explored in this service.

Use a music group or recordings to provide suitable instrumental music to enhance the dramatic presentation of the reading. An experienced choir director might find some suitable choral music for the same purpose.

Old Testament reading

See page 42 for the scripted reading.

See page 42 for the scripted reading.

This is *not* a dramatised reading for the children to perform for the adults. All the parts must be shared out equally across the various age ranges. For example, Jonah could be a teenager and the ship's captain could be an older man; the crew can include females of any age; the narrator could be a woman.

The messenger of God
who ran away

An introduction is given by the minister or the narrator along these lines:

Our story is of the reluctant, and very human, prophet Jonah. It is from the book of the Bible which is named after him, and it was probably written about 600 years before the birth of Jesus. It is not intended that we think of it as history; it is meant to be a parable, like the stories that Jesus told. Now a parable is a story that illustrates an idea; it is a story with a meaning.

When the Jewish people celebrate Yom Kippur, the Day of Atonement, they fast all day to express sorrow for their sins. In the synagogue in the afternoon they read the Book of Jonah and apply it to themselves. Being Jewish, Jesus and the first Christians would have been familiar with this practice, which we are going to imitate now.

A Jewish rabbi would point out to his congregation how Jonah tried to run away from God, turned his back, and, in other words, sinned. This is expressed in the text by the word 'down', which is repeated continually, as you will notice.

Narrator	The word of the Lord came to Jonah. The message was clear.
God	Go at once to the great city of Nineveh. I have heard of the people's wickedness and you are to tell them to repent.
Narrator	Jonah did not want to hear or do what he was asked. Instead he ran away.
Jonah	I'll go to Spain instead. If I go down to Joppa I can find a ship to take me to Tarshish.
Narrator	So Jonah ignored the Lord and went down to Joppa. He paid his fare and went on board ship.
Jonah	This ship is going in the opposite direction to Nineveh, so I can't be made to go there.

Narrator	They were only a few days into their journey when the Lord caused a great wind to blow upon the sea and a terrible storm blew up. It was so bad that the captain and the crew thought the ship was going to break up under the lashing waves and cruel wind.
Various crew members	a. We're going to drown. b. Poseidon, god of the sea, save us. c. Mighty Zeus, Zeus of wind and weather, save us.
Captain	Stop the praying and get this deck cargo overboard. Throw over all the heavy tackle. Get a move on.
Narrator	Meanwhile Jonah had gone down into the hold, where he lay down and fell asleep. The captain, looking for cargo to throw overboard, found Jonah, asleep down in the hold.
Captain	How can you sleep at a time like this? Get up and pray to your God to help. If you pray hard perhaps your God will be kind and we will not all die.
Narrator	The sailors meanwhile were trying to find out who had brought such a terrible punishment on the ship.
Sailor A	You're always unlucky, Jason, it must be your fault.
Sailor B (Jason)	No, it's not. Let's draw lots to find out whose fault it is.
Narrator	So they drew straws or cast lots and, yes, it was clear that Jonah was to blame. They said to him:
Sailor B	Who are you?
Sailor A	Where are you from?
Sailor C	What nationality are you?

Sailor A	What dreadful thing have you done to bring this punishment on all of us?
Jonah	I am a Hebrew; and we Hebrews worship the one true God. We believe that he made the whole world, the sea and the sky.
Narrator	The captain and crew, gathered round, were terrified when they heard this.
Captain	What have you done, then, to upset your God?
Narrator	When the sailors heard that Jonah was running away from what the Lord God had asked him to do, they asked:
Captain	What must we do to make up to your God and stop this dreadful storm?
Jonah	There's only one thing to do. Throw me overboard; then the sea will calm again.
Narrator	The sailors did not want to do this and decided to try rowing with their large sea oars. They struggled hard in the torrential rain for hours and then gave up. Faced with the prospect of throwing Jonah over the side, the captain prayed.
Captain	O Lord, please do not let us all die because of this one man. May we not be found guilty of killing an innocent person. You, O Lord, by your own will, have brought all this about.
Narrator	So the crew heaved Jonah over the side, and he sank down into the lashing waves. Hardly had he disappeared when the wind eased, the waves stopped hammering the ship and the storm passed. The captain and crew were amazed and set about immediately to offer a sacrifice to the one true God. Meanwhile Jonah had sunk down in the sea

and a huge fish swallowed him alive. He remained there, deep in the fish's belly, for three days and three nights. Now, at last, when he was as low as he could get, Jonah prayed.

Jonah In my trouble I called to you, Lord,
and you answered me;
from the depths of the grave
I called for help,
and you listened to my cry.
You hurled me into the deep,
into the heart of the sea,
the currents swirled about me;
all your waves and breakers
swept over me.
I thought I was driven away
out of your sight.
But you brought my life
up from the pit, O Lord my God.
When my life was ebbing away,
I remembered you, Lord,
and my prayer came before you.
What I have promised, I will perform.
Salvation comes from the Lord.

Narrator The Lord commanded the fish, and it vomited Jonah on to dry land. When God spoke again to Jonah, asking him to go to Nineveh, he obeyed immediately and set off for the great city.

Children's song   After the reading of the Gospel (Matthew 12:38-42) the children aged under 12 can be taken aside (to the hall, vestry or similar place) during the address to learn an action song about Jonah (see next page). They will sing it and lead the congregation in the actions when they return immediately following the sermon.

The song goes to the tune of 'London Bridge', and it is easy to work out accompanying actions. The children's leader can work out some beforehand or, better still, get the children to suggest ideas.

Jonah tried to run away
(to the tune of 'London Bridge')

Jonah tried to run away,
run away, run away;
Jonah tried to run away,
far, far away.

Jonah tried to sail away,
sail away, sail away;
Jonah tried to sail away,
far, far away.

Down he went into the sea,
into the sea, into the sea;
down he went into the sea,
down, down, down.

Swallowed alive by a whale,
by a whale, by a whale;
swallowed alive by a whale,
down, deep inside.

Jonah prayed in the whale,
in the whale, in the whale;
Jonah prayed in the whale,
promised to do better.

On the third day out he came,
out he came, out he came;
on the third day out he came,
to obey his God.

Address   The words of Jesus – 'As Jonah was three days and three nights in the belly of a huge fish, so the Son of Man will be three days and three nights in the heart of the earth'– link our dramatised first reading with Easter. There is much in the Jonah story to show us the meaning and purpose of Lent.

Mothering Sunday _____

Background note
Mothering Sunday is celebrated on the fourth Sunday of Lent, which is often the nearest Sunday to 25 March, the feast of the Annunciation. From quite early times this feast day, nine months before Christmas Day, was chosen to celebrate the motherhood of Mary, and by association this came to be a celebration of motherhood in general. So the custom of 'Mother's Day' has developed with visits and gifts for all mothers.

Biblical note
The text of the event that we call the Annunciation, when Mary conceived, is found in Luke 1:26-38. Another text, which is more appropriate for use in Lent, is John 19:25-27.

Visual/decoration
The women's groups in the church should be invited to take responsibility for the decoration of the church on this day. The aim is not just to make the church look attractive but to explore, by any medium they wish (within reason), the concept of 'motherhood'. Hopefully they would not need reminding that the theme should include mothers of teenagers, and grandmothers (all-age motherhood).

Exploring the theme
Pastorally this day is important because of its wide popular appeal, echoed in the secular world. Coming towards the end of Lent, it cuts across the penitential nature of the season. This can either be ignored, in view of the wider pastoral implications (Mark 2:27), or the theme can include the suffering of Mary (and by implication all mothers), as the Passion approaches.

It should, on the other hand, not be a bland 'thank you for mums' day; the original connection with Mary the mother of Jesus should be retained.

Music
The following are suitable hymns:
- Father, I place into your hands
- Now thank we all our God
- He's got the whole world in his hand
- Love divine, all loves excelling
- If I were a butterfly

Readings   Select from the following:

- Genesis 1:26-28, 31a
- Genesis 2:4-9, 15-24
- Genesis 23:1-4, 22
- 1 Samuel 1:20-28
- Ruth 1:8-17, 22
- Proverbs 31:10-31
- 2 Timothy 7:21, 24-27
- Ephesians 5:26-6:4
- Luke 1:26-28
- John 19:23-29
- Mark 10:2-16
- Luke 11:1-13

Alternative reading   The following comes from that celebrated writer, 'Author Unknown'.

When God was creating mothers, he was deep into his sixth day of overtime. An angel appeared and said, 'You're doing a lot of fiddling around on this one.' And God answered, 'Look at the requirement on this order and you'll understand why. She has to be completely washable but not plastic. Have 180 movable parts, each one replaceable. Run on black coffee and leftovers. Have a kiss that can cure anything from a broken leg to a disappointed love affair. And have six pairs of hands.'

The angel shook her head, 'Six pairs of hands? That's not possible even for you, O God.' 'It's not the hands that are causing me problems,' replied the Lord. 'It's the three pairs of eyes mothers are supposed to have.' Asked the angel, 'Are the three pairs of eyes supposed to be on the standard model?' The Lord nodded gravely. 'One pair that sees through closed doors when she asks, "What are you kids doing in there?" – even though she already knows. Another pair in the back of her head that sees what she shouldn't but what she has to know. And, of course, the ones here, in front, that can look at a child when he goofs and reflect, "I understand and I love you," even though she doesn't utter a word.'

'Lord,' said the angel, touching his sleeve gently, 'come to bed. Tomorrow . . . try again.' 'I can't,' said the Lord. 'I'm so close to creating something so similar to myself. Already I have one who heals herself when she is sick, can feed a family of six on one pound of mince, and get a 9-year-old to stay under a shower for an incredible two minutes.'

The angel circled the model of the mother very slowly and sighed, 'It's much too soft, dear God.' 'Soft, yes, but tough too,' said the Lord excitedly. 'You cannot imagine what the mother has to do or endure.' Asked the angel, 'Can it think?' 'Not only think,' said the Creator. 'It can also reason and compromise.'

Finally the angel bent over and ran her fingers across the cheek. 'There's a leak,' she said suddenly. 'I told you that you were trying to fit too much into this model. You can't ignore the stress factor.'

The Lord moved in for a closer look and gently lifted the drop of moisture to his finger where it glistened and sparkled in the light. 'It's not a leak,' God said. 'It's a tear.'

The angel queried, 'A tear? What's that for?' 'It's for joy, sadness, disappointment, compassion, pain, loneliness and pride.' 'You are a genius,' said the angel rapturously. The Lord looked sombre and said, 'I didn't put it there.'

Introduction The giving of flowers is associated with Mothering Sunday. As the congregation enter, young children (rehearsed to do this) can offer a small bunch (three or four flowers) or a single daffodil to each mother (including, of course, grandmothers). Just before the service begins, the mothers can be invited to come forward with their flowers to place them in flower vases arranged in a letter M. At the end of the service the mothers are invited to come forward to receive back their flowers, to take home. After the flowers have been put in the vases, the minister can explain that the M stands for Mary, whose Annunciation and motherhood we are celebrating; and equally the M stands for the motherhood of all those who placed their flowers in the vases.

Address The alternative reading could be read by a teenager at this point. (It is especially relevant for a teenager to do this because of the regular friction that can occur between mothers and their teenage offspring.)

The speaker can comment on the humorous portrait of the model mother and how tough mothers must be for their demanding job. Mothers like to say 'yes' to their children. Sometimes if mistakes are made it is because they say 'yes' too often; there is always the danger of spoiling a child. Mary, the mother of our Saviour, said 'yes' to God on the day we are celebrating, nine months before Christmas day. She accepted God's will for her: 'May it be to me as you have said.' (Luke 1:38)

Serving a family not only involves saying 'yes' to others continually, but so often means saying 'no' to oneself.

Today we say 'thank you' to all mothers for all the sacrifices they have made for the sake of their families.

Easter

Background note

Easter is the greatest and oldest festival and the central focus of our faith. Its importance is emphasised by the long preparation of Lent, Passiontide and the special ceremonies of Holy Week. According to the Anglo-Saxon Church historian, the Venerable Bede, the name 'Easter' originates from the pagan goddess of spring, Eostre.

In the first three centuries it was a commemoration of the Cross and Resurrection. An evolution began in the fourth century with the development of Good Friday and the limiting of the Pascha, the Christian Passover, to the Sunday.

The secular world, in modern times, has made more and more of Christmas for commercial reasons, while it has made less and less of Good Friday and Easter Sunday. But for chocolate eggs, Easter would pass unnoticed by society, and ministers and pastoral leaders have to work hard to reaffirm the centrality and vital importance of this festival of the Lord's death and resurrection.

Biblical note

The Gospel narrative makes it abundantly clear that Jesus deliberately chose the season of the Passover to go up to the Holy City and confront his critics, the Jewish authorities. At the festival celebrating the central event of the Old Covenant – the escape from slavery– Jesus gives a New Covenant, sealed in his blood (Luke 22:20). This final celebration of the Passover, the Last Supper, stands at the decisive frontier between, on the one side, the Jewish Passover and the Old Covenant, and, on the other side, the annual celebration of the Christian Passover and the weekly celebration of the Eucharist.

Visual/decoration

As with Christmas, Churches have their own traditions about Easter which need to be questioned from time to time to see if they still 'work'.

'Festive' and 'joyful' are the themes as we celebrate new life. The flower arrangements should radiate the life and excitement of the wondrous miracle of the Lord's conquest over death. If an Easter garden is considered, why not go for a life-size one? If there are pillars and windowsills, these can be shared out among the church groups, not forgetting the children and young people's groups. Give each a theme: Risen to Life; Light and Life; Born Again; Waters of Life, etc.

Exploring the theme This could be called 'the service of the three Gardens'. The clue is from Paul's insight of the contrast and balance between Adam, the first man, and Christ, the second Adam. A reading of Romans 5:12-19 makes this clear. Verse 19 reads: 'For just as through the disobedience of the one man many were made sinners, so also through the obedience of the one man the many were made righteous.' Obedience is the key which links the Garden of Eden, the Garden of Gethsemane and the Garden of the Empty Tomb.

- In the **Garden of Eden** (however interpreted) we see the first human sin, the sin of disobedience: humans were not prepared to do God's will.

- In the **Garden of Gethsemane** Jesus pleads, 'Please do not ask this suffering of me . . . but not my will, your will be done.' The second Adam accepts God's will.

- In the **Garden of the Tomb**, the Father shows the whole human race that he accepts nothing but simple obedience – 'thy will be done on earth as it is in heaven' – and the obedience of Jesus is rewarded with his resurrection. He is established as Lord and Christ (Acts 2:36).

It is believed by many that in Philippians 2 Paul inserts the words of an early Christian hymn, already well-established in Christian communities, which sums up what we have been saying:

> And being found in appearance as a man, he humbled himself and became obedient to death – death on a cross!
>
> Therefore God exalted him to the highest place and gave him a name that is above every name, that at the name of Jesus every knee should bow, in heaven and on earth and under the earth, and every tongue confess that Jesus Christ is Lord, to the glory of God the Father. (Philippians 2:8-11)

Music Suitable hymns include the following:
- Rejoice in the Lord always
- This is the day
- Alleluia, alleluia, give thanks to the risen Lord
- Jesus Christ is risen today
- Thine be the glory

Readings The Easter readings are provided by the Lectionary. If a service on the theme of the three Gardens is to be followed, these are suitable:
- Genesis 3:1-13
- 1 Corinthians 5:12-22
- Mark 14:32-38 followed by Mark 16:1-7

Introduction   The theme is deeply theological and is the very basis of the Christian faith. Participants will benefit according to their own place on the faith journey. Children may only recognise that there is a link between the Garden of Eden and the death and resurrection of Jesus, but even that is a success, to be built on in the future. More experienced adults may be prompted to meditate upon their need to seek God's will more faithfully in their lives.

To communicate the connection between the three gardens of the theme, the planning group could arrange for three gardens, static displays, to be provided (each one could be the responsibility of a different church group). The largest should be the Resurrection display. A large-scale tomb could be built with live guards asleep outside and real women visiting; such a tableau has been known to work very well.

Alternatively, there could be three mini-plays, each before or after (or in place of) the reading. Or select three part-readings from *The Dramatised Bible*.

Prepare three large white cards. On one draw a large apple, on another an olive tree or an owl, and on the last a butterfly.

Before the service commences, or as part of the introductory rites, the minister shows the cards one by one. (Young people can hold the cards up for the minister.)

- **Apple:** In the Garden of Eden Eve took the fruit from the tree and shared it with Adam. That fruit has traditionally been represented by the apple.

- **Olive tree or owl:** In the Garden of Gethsemane or the Garden of Olives, where Jesus prayed in agony before his Passion, there are olive trees. It was night-time when Jesus prayed in agony, and someone must have seen and recorded what happened, like a wise old owl.

- **Butterfly:** In the Garden of the Empty Tomb there would have been butterflies. The butterfly has been a symbol of the Resurrection since the early years of Christianity.

Readings   The readings should be dramatically presented (see Introduction above).

Children's address   Return to the cards with the three symbols. Each one can be held up by a child and more fully explained, this time linking the apple with the other two. Because Adam and Eve did not do as they were told, they took the apple. In the garden full of olive trees Jesus prayed; he then said 'yes' to what God his Father asked him – the opposite of what Adam and Eve did in their garden. The butterfly emerges from the apparently dead chrysalis to a beautiful new life. The Father rewards Jesus for saying 'yes' to him.

Children's activity During the adult address, the children are asked to select an adult to go with them to a separate place (encourage them not to choose a parent). They are to talk with the adult about how we can be like Jesus and not like Adam (that is, obedient to God's will). Then express this in a drawing or picture.

Adults' address 'Thy kingdom come, thy will be done.' We pray this regularly, but have we understood what we are saying? God's kingdom of love, here and now, and in the future, can only come about by our doing what God asks, here and now.

Adam failed to do God's will and the consequence was humankind's separation from God. The second Adam, after a struggle, was obedient. Notice 'after a struggle': Jesus had prayed, 'Take this suffering away . . . but your will be done.' His struggle and his obedience were rewarded. He was raised, and established as Lord and Christ. Jesus is the man in whom the kingdom has come, because he did God's will.

Only by finding and trying hard to do God's will – it is sometimes a big struggle – will the kingdom come for us and in us.

The children return and present their work to the minister, who shares it with the congregation.

Pentecost

Background note

The Greek word for Pentecost refers to the fiftieth day, being the period of time from the Passover to one of the pilgrim festivals of the Old Covenant, which celebrated the wheat harvest.

Until the fourth century Christians celebrated on this day both the Ascension of the Lord and the coming of the Holy Spirit. In the course of the fourth century a separate day was given over solely to the descent of the Holy Spirit.

The word 'Whitsun' is derived from White Sunday, which was the last day on which those who had been baptised at Easter wore their baptismal tunics or robes.

Biblical note

Pentecost is the birthday of the Church. 'It was not the brain-child of the disciples; it was the work of God. God spoke to its founder members and worked among them in such power that they had no option but to respond to his orders' (John Drane). Acts 2:1-12 speaks of that 'religious experience' that is best described as 'what seemed to be tongues of fire'; a descriptive metaphor very appropriate to what was just about to happen in the first proclamation of the Good News.

Visual/decoration

The predominant colour for the flower arrangements should be red, but orange and yellow can also contribute to remind everyone of the tongues of fire.

If the design and layout of the church permit – that is, if , for example, there are twelve pillars (six on either side) or twelve wall spaces – mount twelve identical posters. They should be at least A3 size, with a very large bright red and yellow flame shape, and can be made by the young people.

A good idea is to announce two weeks beforehand (and remember to explain the idea in the newsletter) that all church-goers, of every age, are invited to bring a small gift wrapped in red paper on Pentecost morning. Guidance will need to be given about the mystery gift, stating that none should cost more than £2 or £3, to avoid embarrassing those who cannot afford much. The planning team may decide to give guidance about the type of gift – for example, a small box of chocolates; a small dried-flower arrangement; a home-made badge or brooch made from modelling material. The team could also buy a small number of gifts, which will be wrapped and ready at the back of the church, available for anyone who turns up on Pentecost Sunday unprepared. After an introductory word by the minister/leader at the commencement of the service, or after the Gospel reading, the congregation are asked to leave their places and present their gift to someone they do not know, or do not know well. (The Spirit of Love makes us all members of one another.)

Another idea, which has worked well and sparked discussion, is to ask all church members to attend that day wearing something red.

Exploring the theme   Any of the symbols of Pentecost can be taken and developed. Here we are using the symbol of fire.

Music   Hymns might include some of the following:
- Breathe on me, breath of God
- Come, Holy Ghost
- Come down, O love divine
- Spirit of the living God
- The Spirit lives to set us free

The choir could sing:
- Christ is the world's true light (Stanton)
- Lord, give thy Holy Spirit (Tallis)

Readings   The readings for Pentecost are:
- Genesis 11:1-9
- Acts 2:1-11
- 1 Corinthians 12:3-7, 12-13
- John 20:19-23 or John 14:15-26

Where possible, use *The Dramatised Bible* for the Acts passage. A dramatic effect can be achieved by building up a cacophony of noise. The young people would enjoy doing this at the back of the church. (If necessary, warn the rest of the congregation that it is part of the service and not some disrespectful behaviour!) The talking can start quietly and build up. At the words in Acts 2, verse 11 – 'We hear them declaring the wonders of God in our own tongues' – all noise stops. Everyone then reads or says together, 'The Spirit unites us in the language of love.' Or, without any introduction, the hymn 'The Spirit lives to set us free' is sung.

Introduction In the Visual section it was suggested that a couple of weeks beforehand all the congregation could be invited to wear something red for this service and/or bring a small gift to present to someone they do not know. This could take place after the Gospel, when a link can be made with God's free gift of his Spirit to us, and how this gift leads us into loving service.

In the Visual section it was suggested that a couple of weeks beforehand all the congregation could be invited to wear something red for this service and/or bring a small gift to present to someone they do not know. This could take place after the Gospel, when a link can be made with God's free gift of his Spirit to us, and how this gift leads us into loving service.

Four volunteers are required: an elderly man, a teenage boy, a small girl and a middle-aged mother. Each is to prepare a few words about fire. The following are only examples. The man could speak of using a bonfire in his garden to burn rubbish. The boy might speak, perhaps, of his achievement as a Scout, learning how to light a fire with one match (do Scouts still do such 'interesting' things?), or describe the sense of fraternity around a campfire. The small girl may speak of how she has been warned of the dangers of playing with matches, or of her fear of fire. The mother could talk about cooking on an open fire on some occasion, or on a gasfire.

Address After the Gospel the four 'volunteers' come forward. The minister then speaks of the symbolism of the colour red, related to the 'fire' of the Holy Spirit. The four people then make their presentations. The minister proceeds to the qualities of fire: fire as a cleansing power; fire which gives light; fire which can frighten; the warmth of fire, and so on. The coming of the Holy Spirit lit up the minds of the Apostles, clearing their minds of their fears and misunderstandings, and warmed their hearts with love.

The same can happen to us if we welcome the Spirit. All the ancient hymns to the Holy Spirit begin with the word 'Veni' (Come), and that must be our constant prayer: 'Come, Holy Spirit, enlighten our minds and warm our hearts by the fire of your love.'

Trinity Sunday

Background note

This festival is different in character from those which commemorate the historical events of salvation. It is always held on the first Sunday after Pentecost and it was introduced officially as part of the Church calendar in the fourteenth century, to mark the end of the cycle commemorating the life of Christ and the descent of the Holy Spirit.

The day was especially popular in England, perhaps because Thomas à Becket was consecrated bishop on that day in 1162. Formerly, from the ancient Sarum Rite and the book of Common Prayer, Sundays were reckoned after Trinity and not after Pentecost.

Today it acts as a powerful reminder, if celebrated in a way that really draws it to everyone's attention, that the Christian life is lived for the Father, by the power of the Holy Spirit, through the saving work of Christ our Lord. We are not Unitarians nor are we so charismatic that we forget the Father and the Son.

Trinity Sunday is the key festival of all-age worship, for it reminds us of the 'community' or 'family' life in God. As this day comes in the early summer, in May or June, it is an ideal weekend on which to have a full day all-age event, perhaps out of doors.

Biblical note

The central doctrine of Christian theology is held to be a mystery, in the sense that it can neither be known by unaided reason, apart from revelation, nor be cogently demonstrated by reason after it has been revealed. The word 'Trinity' (Tri-unity) is not found in the Bible and was first used in the second century; however, the teaching is held to be explicit and implicit in Scripture, for example in the baptismal words of Matthew 28:19 and at the baptism of Jesus (Matthew 3:16). The Last Supper speech of Jesus (John 14:11, 16f) expresses the belief very clearly. (See also 1 Peter 1:2 and 2 Corinthians 13:14.)

Visual/decoration

The creativity of flower arrangers is stretched by this festival which defies the use of the imagination. If three strong colours can be used that remain separate at the top of the arrangement but come to blend together at the bottom, this might convey the right effect.

The most suitable visual is the icon by Andrei Rublev, painted in the fifteenth century and obtainable in poster form. If this is used, a few minutes should be set aside to give a simple explanation. (My book, *Gateway to the Trinity*, St Paul Publications, explains the icon. The poster and book are both available from St Paul Multimedia Productions – contact details on page 111.) The icon could be the central feature of the floral arrangement.

Exploring the theme The inner 'family' life of God is mysterious and unapproachable through the human imagination; however, the existence of the human family aids the understanding. A grasp of the simple but profound union of love between husband and wife, made visible in their first child, is as near as anyone can get to this mystery. The image and example of the human family could therefore be used in this service.

Music The following hymns are suitable:
- Father, we adore you
- Holy, holy, holy
- Holy, holy, holy! Lord God almighty

The choir could sing:
- Holy, holy, holy (Palestrina)

Readings Choose from the following:
- Isaiah 6:1-8
- Exodus 34:4-6, 8-9
- Deuteronomy 4:32-34, 39-40
- Ephesians 1:3-14
- Romans 8:14-17
- 2 Corinthians 13:11-13
- John 14:8-17
- John 3:16-18
- Matthew 28:16-20

Introduction Get together three family groups of mother, father and child. Groups, ideally, should span the age range. For example, the first family group could consist of a young couple with a baby (the younger the better), the second group with a 10-year-old daughter or son, and the last group could be an elderly couple with a grown-up son or daughter. These nine people should be as involved in the service as possible – reading, taking the offerings, for example.

The presentation of the three families could come at the opening of the service or immediately after the Gospel, as an introduction to the sermon or address.

Each couple should stand side by side, with their child in front, between them. The minister introduces the nine people, group by group. The comment could then include the following points.

We have here three families. They are of varying ages, but are still the family unit. The baby is totally dependent, the school child is growing in independence, and the grown-up is totally independent, yet there is still the bond of family love and mutual respect.

The love of husband and wife for one another is visible to everyone in the existence of the child. In the family of God that we call the Trinity, the total love of the first person (the Father) for the second person (the Word who was made flesh), and the return of that love, is made visible in the Spirit of Love, the third person of the Trinity. So the best image to help us understand the Trinity is the human family; three examples of which you can see before you. (It is advisable to avoid using the term 'son' of the second person in this explanation, because it will confuse.)

Address   The ideal visual aid for the sermon or address is the icon by Rublev. (It is recommended to read first the very short book, *Gateway to the Trinity* – see page 60.)

The family groups, already described, would make an ideal starting point. Don't attempt philosophical or theological explanations; the Trinity as a union of love, similar to the human family, is the most helpful approach. Ordinary family people can enter into the mystery of love, without any need for mathematical confusion, with talk of one in three and three in one. The numerous Scripture references given above will demonstrate the Holy Trinity in action.

Harvest

Background note

Although there were Jewish precedents, the Christian Church had no Harvest Festival, as such, until relatively recent history. In England, from Saxon times until the Reformation, there was Lammas (Loaf Mass) on 1 August, with the blessing of bread made from the first ripe corn. In 1843 the Revd R. S. Hawker, vicar of Morwenstow in Cornwall, revived the Lammas custom and extended the thanksgiving for the whole harvest. The revival spread into the nonconformist Churches and, more recently, the Roman Catholic Church.

Biblical note

The Old Testament called for a celebration called Shavuoth, the Feast of Weeks or Pentecost, which took place seven weeks after Passover. It was the wheat harvest festival to thank God for the first fruits of the harvest. 'Count off seven weeks from the time you begin to put the sickle to the standing corn. Then celebrate the Feast of Weeks to the Lord your God by giving a freewill offering' (Deuteronomy 16:9). In later times, after the establishment of synagogues up and down the country, it came to be called Pentecost and was associated with spiritual harvest and the giving of the Law on Mount Sinai. The early Christians do not appear to have commemorated the harvest, perhaps because they were expecting the return of the Lord at any time.

Visual/decoration

Most churches have their customary way of decorating for this celebration, but it should not become routine. We should not lose sight of our link with the soil, which was expressed more in former times when more churchgoers were agricultural workers. Harvest not only expresses thanks 'up' to God but reminds us of our link 'down' with the earth and the cycle of the seasons. Gardening tools – spades, forks, rakes – can be brought into church and incorporated into vegetable and floral arrangements.

Nor should we forget the harvest from the sea. This is particularly important in a seaside town or port. If windows, ledges and pillars are being decorated, there can be fruitful place for a fishing net hung with paper cutouts of various fish.

Exploring the theme

Harvest thanksgiving: there is no 'thanks' without 'giving'. On Mothering Sunday thanks are expressed by the giving of gifts. The central act of Christian worship, the Eucharist

('Thanksgiving') expresses gratitude to God and involves the gifts of bread and wine and God's gift of his own Son. At Harvest Festival we say 'thank you' for God's goodness with the gifts we offer for those in need. (Every town and city has homeless people, or a women's refuge, as well as needy elderly.)

Music Any suitable hymn or song of thanksgiving can be used, such as the following:

- Come, you thankful people, come
- Fill your hearts with joy
- Great is thy faithfulness

Readings
- Deuteronomy 8:1-10   Genesis 1:1-3, 24-31a
- Acts 14:13-17   Timothy 6:6-10
- Luke 12:16-31   John 6:27-35

Alternative reading 'Harvest Home', from chapter 15 of *Lark Rise* by Flora Thompson could be read:

> At last, in the cool dusk of an August evening, the last load of corn was brought in, with a nest of merry boys' faces among the sheaves on the top of the yellow and blue painted farm wagons drawn by the big cart-horses and the men walking alongside with pitchforks on their shoulders. As they passed along the roads they shouted, 'Harvest home. Harvest home. Merry, merry, merry, harvest home,' and women came to their cottage gates and waved, the few passers-by looked up and smiled their congratulations. The joy and pleasure of the labourers in their task well done . . . They loved the soil and rejoiced in their work and skill in bringing forth the fruits of the soil, and 'harvest home' put the crown on their year's work.

Introduction It would be interesting to try to dramatise that passage from *Lark Rise*, using people of all ages and bringing out the huge difference between harvest celebrations of a century ago in England and today. One option is to use this passage after the Gospel reading and before the address or sermon, forming part of it.

Before the service people of various ages who are willing to take part could be given items bought in the local supermarket. They need to be chosen carefully; the intention is to demonstrate how food that makes up our modern diet comes from many different countries. In contrast, one hundred years ago the people could only eat local food that was in season, or had been preserved by methods like salting, bottling or pickling.

At the appropriate time those with the grocery items from abroad can be invited to stand and tell everyone what they have and where it comes from. A number of teaching points can be made of this.

Later in the service the same people, of varied ages, could take part in a thank-you litany; for example:

Minister
Lord God, our creator, provider and sustainer,
we thank you for all your gifts
and for the people who grow, harvest and supply to our shops
the food which we buy for our needs.
First person (holding up food item)
We thank you for tea from Sri Lanka.
Second person
We thank you for oranges from Israel.
(. . . *and so on*)

Concluding prayer
Father of all,
our cupboards and larders are full of the fruits of the earth
from every corner of the world you have given us.
We sincerely thank you for such bounty
and ask that those who grow and supply this food for our benefit
may receive a just reward for their efforts,
so that all your people, rich and poor,
may together be able to thank you.
Amen.

Offering of the gifts
Apart from those gifts which are used to decorate the church, the people may be encouraged to bring a gift or gifts for homeless people, the local women's refuge or a similar local charity. If it is a eucharistic service the ideal time for these to be presented is when the bread and wine are brought to the altar.

It should not just be the children who carry the gifts in procession and present them to the minister. This should be an all-age activity, so that the whole community is represented.

Address
See Introduction above.

Conclusion of the service
A representative of the organisation or group which is to benefit from the gifts could be invited to the service to thank the community.

All Saints

Background note

Celebrating Saints' days and 'All Saints' is yet another way in which the Church celebrates the Paschal (Easter) mystery. Those Christians who have lived, suffered and died as witnesses of the Risen Christ are brought to us as examples, drawing all to the Father through Christ.

So many martyrs and non-martyrs died in the early years, and since, that a common festival was instituted. At the beginning of the fifth century a day for All Martyrs was first observed on Easter Friday. The Easter connection was lost when in AD 835 the feast day was transferred to 1 November, with the title 'All Saints'.

Biblical note

The biblical foundation of this festival is found in the promises of Jesus (Matthew 19:28) to those who have served him. The idea that the dead may intercede for the living is found in the parable of Dives (the rich man) and Lazarus (Luke 16:19-31). The idea of saints as more than past heroes to admire and imitate, but surrounding and supporting us on our pilgrimage, is found in Hebrews 12:1. Revelation speaks particularly of the martyrs in 6:9f and 7:14-17.

However, the principle basis of the practice is Paul's teaching of the mystical Body of Christ, in which all members have their particular office (Romans 12:4-8) as fellow citizens with the saints.

Visual/decoration

In a suitable place, beneath the pulpit or to one side of the altar, a small 'house' can be constructed by the youth group or older children. Made of building blocks of small cardboard boxes covered in red crêpe paper, or painted red, with a roof, it need not stand more than about 3 feet high. Around it arrange vases of white chrysanthemums. (The colours used must be red and white.)

Before or during the introduction, or as part of the address or sermon, the symbolism of the decoration needs to be explained. Briefly, today is the festival of those who belong to the household of the Christian faith, those of us who are alive here and now and those who are alive with God. Baptism (the white flowers) unites us all, as children of God. Many in the past, and today in places like the Sudan, have shed their blood for their faith (the red of the house).

Exploring the theme   This festival is a celebration of the Communion of Saints, or the mystical Body of Christ. This day does not celebrate canonised saints or make special mention of any of them; today celebrates the good lives of the millions of Christians (of all branches of the Christian family) who are now with God. Particularly we can recall saintly members of our own family and our community. We thank God for the inspiring example of their lives and ask that they will intercede for us with God.

Music   Any hymn or song which brings out the 'family' nature of the Church, such as the following:

- For all the saints
- Father, I place into your hands
- He's got the whole world in his hand
- Seek ye first
- Thy hand, O God, has guided

Readings

- Revelation 7:2-4, 9-14
- Romans 12:3-9
- 1 John 3:1-3
- 1 Corinthians 12:12-13, 27-31
- Matthew 5:1-12

Introduction   Make up a list of past members of the community who have been lovingly remembered for their devout lives and service to the community. This can be done either by the planning group, or by asking the community in preceding weeks for proposed names. (Tact may be necessary to avoid giving offence; the person must have had some recognition within the community.)

Choose representatives of every age group, from the youngest that can walk unaided, to the eldest parishioner.

The names on the list are distributed to those of this group who are old enough to read. The representatives enter with the minister(s) and are involved in the introductory part of the service.

After the opening explanation of the visual/decoration, or in place of it, the representatives of the community are introduced. They are then invited, in the name of the local community, to read out the names of honoured past members. The reason for doing this is explained.

Intercessions

These will be led by the representatives of the community who entered with the minister(s). If it fits the traditions of the community, incense can be used. Live charcoals need to be left standing, in a suitable receptacle (for example, a thurible), before the altar or communion table. Beside it lies a container of incense with a spoon. One of the younger representatives is invited to come forward at the appropriate moment to place a spoonful of incense on the coals.

Reader
'The twenty-four elders fell down before the Lamb.
Each one had a harp and they were holding golden bowls full of incense, which are the prayers of the saints.'
(Revelation 5:8)

(Representative steps forward and sprinkles the incense on the coals)

Reader
'Worthy is the Lamb, who was slain,
to receive power and wealth and wisdom and strength
and honour and glory and praise.'
(Revelation 5:12)

Minister
Almighty Father, we set before you, like incense,
our intercessions and offer them to you,
in the name of the Lamb of God,
who ever lives to make intercession to you on our behalf.

Community representative
For those who lead our church/parish community;
may they be inspired by the saintly example
of those who have gone before.

Response by all
May our prayer be set before you like incense.
(Psalm 141:2)

Community representative
For those who have been recently baptised
or who are preparing for baptism;
may the baptised and honoured members of our community
who have gone before
intercede for them.

Response by all
May our prayer be set before you like incense.

Community representative
For our young people;
may they receive a good example in living
from all the present members of our community
and be inspired by the lives of those who have gone before.

Response by all
May our prayer be set before you like incense.

(This format is continued to encompass the needs of the community.)

Children's address

The following simple story is a very effective starting point.

A little girl was with her family in a group of tourists who were being shown round one of England's great cathedrals. As the guide was explaining an ancient tomb nearby, the girl was staring at a great stained window through which the summer sun was streaming, bathing the cathedral floor in colour. As the group was about to move on she asked in a shrill clear voice, 'Who are those people in the pretty window?'

'Those are the saints,' the guide replied.

That night, as she was undressing for bed, she told her mother, 'I know who the saints are.'

'Do you, dear?' replied her mother. 'Who are they?'

'They're the people who let the light shine through.'

Any other address or sermon could well begin with a story or anecdote from the lives of those whose names have been read out.

SECTION TWO

All-age Activities to Illustrate Hymns

Introduction Ideally all worship by a community is all-age worship. In practice this is rarely so. This section offers ideas on how to add a simple all-age dimension to the regular act of worship. Little preparation is necessary, and not all examples involve an action.

All-age activities to illustrate hymns are very useful when there is little time to consult a team and prepare a full service but there is a desire to provide an all-age dimension to the standard Sunday service. The following suggestions are only guides to help the pastoral practitioner formulate his or her own ideas.

Simple participatory activities are described for the following hymns. They can form part of all-age events, or be slipped in to the regular service to involve everyone present.

Theme	*Hymn*
Abandonment to God	Father, I place into your hands
All God's creatures	All things bright and beautiful
The Bread of Life	Bread is blessed and broken
Christian meditation	Be still, for the presence of the Lord
The Eucharist	This is my body
Forgiveness	God forgave my sin
God's family	Bind us together, Lord
God's universe	Immortal, invisible, God only wise
The Holy Name	At the name of Jesus
The Holy Spirit	Breathe on me, Breath of God
Individual dignity	Lord, the light of your love is shining
In God's hands	He's got the whole world in his hand
Intercession for the world	For the healing of the nations
Jesus, our Saviour	God is love: his the care
Joy in living	Rejoice in the Lord always
The light of Christ's love	Lord, the light of your love is shining
Listening to God	Listen, let your heart keep seeking
Living for God	Lead us, heavenly Father, lead us
Love one another	A new commandment
Names of God	Father, we love you

71

Respecting creation	All creatures of our God and King
Returning to God	Amazing grace
Spiritual growth	Be still and know that I am God
Spreading the light of Christ	Colours of day
Trust in God	Do not be afraid
Welcoming the Holy Spirit	Come, Holy Ghost *or* Come, Holy Spirit

Abandonment to God   *Father, I place into your hands*

The previous week, or earlier the same day, the children can do some work on the theme 'hands': how we use our hands in God's service and to help others. If they have drawn round and coloured their own hands these can be shown to all present. Alternatively, and if the setting is appropriate and the recording available, the old Max Bygraves song 'You need hands' could be played.

If neither of the above is possible or suitable, individuals can be invited to come forward and speak of how their hands are vital in their work; for example, someone who works all day at a word processor, a surgeon who operates, the mother of a large family, or an ambulance man.

After making the link between working with our hands and placing our lives in God's hands, copies of the following prayer of Charles de Foucauld might be given out.

> Father,
> I abandon myself into your hands;
> do with me what you will.
> Whatever you may do, I thank you;
> I am ready for all, I accept all.
> Let only your will be done in me,
> and in all your creatures –
> I wish no more than this, O Lord.
>
> Into your hands I commend my soul;
> I offer it to you with all the love of my heart,
> for I love you, Lord,
> and so need to give myself,
> to surrender myself into your hands,
> without reserve, and with boundless confidence,
>   for you are my Father.

After the prayer has been read together or by one person, the hymn may be sung.

All God's creatures   *All things bright and beautiful*

This is suitable on the Sunday nearest to 4 October, the feast day of St Francis of Assisi. On the Sunday before, everyone (not just children) could be encouraged to bring their easy-to-bring pets (like goldfish and hamsters – dogs too, if the community is agreeable). Several people can come forward to say a word about their pet – its age, why it has its name, for example. Then say a few words about God's creation, or read Genesis 2:19-20, with a simple commentary. The hymn may follow.

The Bread of Life   *Bread is blessed and broken*

You will need several different types of bread – loaves, rolls, wholemeal, white. If possible, include unleavened matzos or pitta bread.

Show them and explain that, although they look different and are in different forms, they are all bread, the staff of life. Then show the unleavened bread and explain how this is used at the Jewish Passover and in Jewish ritual meals. The matzos can be broken up at this point and the children can help to distribute it. The hymn can now be sung.

Christian meditation   *Be still, for the presence of the Lord*

Ask for total silence and stillness. 'Be still and know that I am God'; no music, no movement, a still church. Then ask everyone to sit up straight with backs against the back support, feet apart and hands in laps. (When this is tried in schools, amazingly children like doing it.) There should be a large lighted candle, a picture, an arrangement of flowers or something similar that can act as a focal point. Ask everyone to look intently on the focal point and try to hear any sounds in the distance – these must now be rejected. Everyone breathes in slowly, hold, and out slowly . . . the familiar meditation routine. Continue for about five minutes, then sing the hymn.

The Eucharist   *This is my body*

This activity is suitable for a Eucharist or Communion service which is also a church parade service. Have at hand one of the flags which has been presented at the commencement of the service and also the bread and the wine.

A Guide or a Scout brings the flag (from wherever the colours are placed) and, in a loud voice, says, 'This flag is a symbol of our company and of our loyalty to the Guide/Scout Movement. We take and try to keep the Guide/Scout promise.'

The minister replies, 'This bread, with this wine, is the symbol of our company or community, as Christians. Christ has made a promise to be always with us. This symbol reminds us of his promises to us and our promise to be faithful to him. Our God is a God of Promise and we are the people of that Promise.'

The representative Guide/Scout then returns to their seat and the minister can enlarge upon the theme of being a company or community of Christians with the Eucharist at its centre, which sustains us spiritually as we try to live by the promise. Sing the hymn.

Forgiveness   *God forgave my sin*

A long roll of paper (the blank side of a spare roll of wallpaper is perfect) is required with the word 'Forgive' printed in large letters seven times, spaced out generously one below the other. Beneath these is a space and then 'Without end' written below. The paper is then rolled up. An adult reader is also required. Comment on how difficult it is to forgive, quoting a topical case: how often should we forgive? Hold the paper to view and reveal the word 'Forgive'. The reader now reads Matthew 18:21-22. The paper is slowly unrolled by young people to reveal all seven words gradually. The last one is followed by a space (suspense) then 'Without end'. The hymn is then sung.

God's family   *Bind us together, Lord*

You will need a house brick, a cauliflower (or similar vegetable) and a branch from a rose bush (or some similar bush or tree). Ask, 'Which is the odd one out?' and encourage replies from all age groups. If no one gets it right – they must give the reason why one is odd – then read John 15:1-8, as a clue.

The answer is the vegetable, because it grows and exists on its own; it is complete in itself. The house brick, on the other hand, forms part of a wall and the branch belongs to a whole plant. We too, as Christians, belong to one another, as members of the family of God. We are 'bricks' in the house of God or 'branches' of the vine. The hymn is now sung.

God's universe   *Immortal, invisible, God only wise*

First ask the young people, 'Have any of you recently seen a video or film about aliens or space?' After listening to the replies, the next question is aimed at the adults: 'Is there anyone who studies or likes to read about space and astronomy?' Following their response, give out these passages to readers of different ages.

a. Let our minds soar. Let us stand in spirit at the margent of the universe and travel in through the galaxies of stars, the clusters of planets, stretching beyond the limits of sight, sown like seed across the plains of darkness.

b. Let us travel at the speed of light, 186 million miles a second, through 15,000 million light years, past stars vaster in size than the whole of our own solar system, through unimaginable distance, unimaginable fire and cold, searching for that speck we call our world, like a speck of sand upon the ocean bed.

c. And it is there, a warm jewel in the womb of night. So tiny, so vulnerable, so dependent, frailer than a cockleshell in the seas round Cape Horn. Dependent upon its master and its own dependent, man.

d. And from out in infinite space we descend, down, down, down to our own town (city / village); to one district, one area, one building – this church.

(The readings are from *Fields of Praise* by John Harriott)

Then ask, 'How do you feel, after those readings?' Very small and insignificant; humbled and of little worth? Whatever we feel, God loves and cares for each one of us, made in his image and likeness. The hymn can now be sung.

The Holy Name   *At the name of Jesus*

Hold up a teddy bear, or a doll, and speak about the bear / doll's name. Then ask those present, adults as well as children, to confess if they have or once had a favourite teddy or doll. It is important to name a teddy or doll – or a pet – because the bond between you and the toy or pet is closer and more personal once a name is given. Names of people often mean something (give examples). The name 'Jesus' was quite common in New Testament time; that's why he was called Jesus of Nazareth, to distinguish him from other men of the same name. Our English 'Jesus' comes from the Hebrew *Yehosua*, or Joshua. It means 'God saves', so you could say the word 'Jesus' means 'saviour' – which of course he was for us. Sing the hymn.

The Holy Spirit   *Breathe on me, Breath of God*

This activity is particularly suitable for Pentecost time. Give out, randomly, to a variety of people (not just children) twelve red balloons. Ask those with balloons to blow them up and hold them. Comment that a balloon only becomes what it is intended to be when it is filled with breath or air. Release your balloons (have fun returning them to their owners): now your red balloons look withered and spent. It is the same with us. The breath of the Holy Spirit fills us with life and makes us the type of people God intended us to be. Without the Spirit we are like a withered balloon. Why red balloons, and why twelve? Red is the colour associated with the Holy Spirit, and twelve for the twelve Apostles who were the first to receive the Spirit on the day of Pentecost. Now sing the hymn.

Individual dignity   *Lord, the light of your love is shining*

This activity is suitable for Pentecost time. Give out a number of candles randomly to a variety of people – the candles must all have different sizes, shapes and colours. Comment on how different each candle is, and how different each person holding the candle is: different ages, different genders, roles in life, and so on. Then say, 'With this one flame (a lit taper) I will come and light each one of the candles.' Having done so, comment that now all candles have the same size flame, giving the same light, regardless of the size, colour or shape of each candle.

It is exactly the same with us; the fire of the Holy Spirit comes to 'light us up' regardless of our age, our size, our place in society and career. The Spirit is the same for all. God is not interested in what age we are, what colour we are, what social class we belong to. He only wants us to be alight with his love and a living witness to the love of God. Now sing the hymn.

In God's hands   *He's got the whole world in his hand*

Place in full view a large globe of the world. (To obtain one, if necessary, put a request in the church / parish weekly newsletter.) Ask a child to come out and show everyone where the British Isles is. Now ask an adult to come forward and point out where Greece is. Then ask the question, 'What was the name of the Greek god of mythology who was a Titan and was condemned to hold up the heavens or the globe?' The answer is Atlas. Make the link between the Greek god and a book, or the globe which shows the countries of the world. God is like

Atlas. He holds up the world, he has the whole universe in his hand. Everything that was, and is, and will be, comes from him. Sing the hymn.

Intercession for the world

For the healing of the nations

Bring out a small pile of newspapers and, picking up selected copies, read out a disturbing headline about crime, war, economic problems, for example. (Alternatively, a number of readers, from their places in the congregation, read out a startling news headline.) After a short comment about the prevalence of bad news about and from our world, and our need to intercede to our Loving Father for the troubles of society, the hymn may be sung.

Jesus, our Saviour

God is love: his the care

Two or three popular newspapers, local or national, are needed. Draw attention to several human stories in the papers, and speak of the insatiable curiosity that people have about the lives and affairs of others. Stories suited to youngsters as well as adults should be included.

Comment on the fact that everyone present has a story to tell, of hard times, of exciting events, of painful experiences. While this is true, Christians are aware of their total dependence upon God and his loving providence. Our greatest story is of how Jesus has been our rescuer, our Saviour, on so many occasions in life and is the Saviour of all humanity. The hymn is now sung.

Joy in living

Rejoice in the Lord always

This activity needs an adult or a child dressed as a clown, or a doll in clown's clothes. If there is a real clown who can take part, just for a few minutes, all the better. Now talk about 'clowning for God'. There is an Anglican priest who is a professional clown and he is in great demand in leading workshops and worship. His book, *Fools Rush In*, shows how 'God chose the foolish things of this world to shame the wise'.

There is a Holy Fools Association of Christian clowns in this country with more than 200 members.

'God is infinite fun' and wants us to be happy. Joy is one of the gifts of the Holy Spirit and a spirit of joy is possessed by all those who come close to God. Now sing the hymn.

The light of Christ's love

Lord, the light of your love is shining

Give out an assortment of batteries, of all sizes and shapes. Ask a child, 'What have I given to you?' Comment on the use of batteries in flash cameras, radios and so on. Ask adults for ideas on sources of power before batteries were invented (gas supply, oil lamps, for example). Modern battery-powered torches are the nearest equivalent to the hand-held oil lamps at the time of Jesus. As Christians, our source of energy, our power of love, is from God himself.

Listening to God

Listen, let your heart keep seeking

(This is a good one for a small group of young people to introduce with a short role-play.)

A man sits on a chair, right of centre, reading a newspaper; a woman stands at an ironing board, pretending to iron, left of centre; a teenager enters carrying a school bag. 'Dad, could you . . .' Father interrupts, 'Ask your Mother.' Teenager turns to the woman: 'Mum, could you . . .' Mother interrupts, 'Not now, dear, I'm listening to the Archers.' Teenager throws down the bag and shouts, 'Yeah, but you don't listen to me!' And storms off.

It is the frequent complaint of young people that their parents don't listen to them. We must not be like those parents, deaf to God when he speaks to us. Now the hymn may be sung.

Living for God

Lead us, heavenly Father, lead us

You will need a house brick and a wide plank of wood or a sheet of plywood. Position the plank at a 45 degree angle, propped against a chair or table. Hold the brick in your hand and ask, 'What will happen if I place this brick at the top of this slide?' Yes, it will slide down. Is it easy to stop? No; possible, but not easy.

It is the same with our lives. We develop bad habits, laziness about our prayers, occasional lies and half-truths. We slide, and it is not easy to stop. The only answer is to take a firm grip on ourselves (match words to action of firmly holding brick) and every day resolve to offer ourselves and all that we are to God our Father, for he is the only one who can 'stop the brick'. Sing the hymn.

Love one another   *A new commandment*

Hold up a book of instructions and explain that they came from inside the cardboard box, when your new computer (dishwasher/washing machine or whatever) was delivered. It tells you what to do, how to plug in and use it properly. If you follow the rules given to you by the manufacturers all will be well. Your new computer (or whatever) will run happily for years.

God gave the human race some instructions or rules for a happy life; we call them the Ten Commandments. Jesus gave us the commandment that we should love one another; and if we try to do that, we will find that life will run more happily. Now sing the hymn.

Names of God   *Father, we love you*

The children and young people need to prepare large sheets of paper or posters with a title of God written clearly in large print. Have as many as possible – for example The Lord, The Almighty, The All-powerful, The All-knowing, Creator – but they must not include the title 'Father' or 'Abba'. The posters are brought out one by one, and shown to everyone. Ask the adults which name is missing. Comment that the Islamic faith has ninety-nine names for God, but not one of them is 'Father', the title the Son of God himself gave us. Now sing the hymn.

Respecting creation   *All creatures of our God and King*

A quantity of playdough needs to be prepared (recipe on page 111). Give everyone a small piece, and ask them to make any animal or creature of their choice. While they are doing this, talk about St Francis of Assisi and his love of nature.

Then read the following:

The end was fast approaching. Two days before his death he asked to be stripped of all his clothes, and to be put on the ground that he might die in the arms of Lady Poverty.

It was on the night of 3 October 1226 that he breathed his last, praising God to the end. With his songs were mingled those of the little birds he loved so well, for we are told that a great multitude of larks came above the roof of the house where he lay, and, flying a little way off, made a circle round the roof, and by their sweet singing seemed to be praising the Lord along with him.

(From an ancient source)

Now go round the children and admire their playdough creations, asking what they are. Remind everyone that as the children have made their own animals, so God has made us and all creatures. We all owe praise to God. The hymn is now sung.

Returning to God   *Amazing grace*

Before the service hide something – a familiar hymn book, for example – somewhere in the church.

Tell the children that you have lost it so they can go and find it for you. While the children are away hunting for the object, ask the adults to think about what happens and what they do when they lose their car keys or house keys. An individual might be encouraged to tell of such an occasion. When the children return, speak about losing and finding things, how worried we get, the problems it causes.

At this point you could read the story Jesus told about the lost coin (Luke 15:8-10) or the lost sheep (Luke 15:1-7), after which the hymn can be sung.

Spiritual growth   *Be still and know that I am God*

Obtain a packet of seeds (beetroot is quite good for this) and put one in the palm of each person's hand. Paul says, 'Never grow weary of doing good' (Galatians 6:9). The seed is very small and it looks quite dead, but we know that if it is put into the ground, watered and kept warm, it will grow. However, there will be a long time when all is 'still', when nothing appears to be happening, before it gives out a shoot and grows into a plant. The Christian life is like that; it needs us to be still, to have patience; it needs light and water and warmth. It needs nurturing or it will fail. Patience and perseverance will bring a harvest. Paul says, 'Let us not become weary in doing, for at the proper time we will reap a harvest if we do not give up.' Now sing the hymn.

Spreading the light of Christ

Colours of day

Standing very prominently and with exaggerated show, strike a match and light a candle. Ask the children, 'What if I had set fire to a pile of old newspapers? What would have happened?' One flame can destroy a whole building, like this church, or can simply light a candle. A lighted match gives power. We who possess the light of Christ's love have power. We can keep the light – the fire – hidden or we can let it blaze out for others to see and see by. The hymn can now be sung.

Trust in God

Do not be afraid

Ask a young person in the congregation, 'What frightens you?' (The answer might be 'spiders' or 'the dark'.) Ask several more children the same question. Then ask an adult, 'What is your first name? Do you know if it has a meaning?' (For example, Sarah means 'princess'.) Ask several other adults the same question.

Now tell this short story.

A little boy was afraid of the dark and asked to sleep in his parents' bedroom with them. He woke in the night and called, 'Daddy.' His father replied, 'What is it? Are you all right?' The boy replied, 'Is your face towards me, Daddy?' 'Yes, Thomas,' the father replied. 'Good,' said the boy, 'now I know I'm all right.' And he went back to sleep.

'Is your face towards me?' God knows each of us personally by name; we can address him as 'Abba' – Daddy – and whatever we fear, his face is turned towards us. His name and his presence dispel fear. The hymn can now follow.

Welcoming the Holy Spirit

Come, Holy Ghost or *Come, Holy Spirit*

Holding up an actual invitation card, or a make-believe one, speak about how exciting it can be to receive an invitation to a wedding, surprise party or celebration. The card will say, 'You are invited to . . .' You are asked to come to the special event. The card will probably carry the letters 'RSVP', which asks you to reply, to accept the invitation.

Then point out that God is always inviting us to respond to his love. We too should invite the Holy Spirit to come to us, to deepen our knowledge and our love. All the famous and ancient hymns to the Holy Spirit start with the word 'Veni', which means 'Come'. The hymn can now be sung.

SECTION THREE
Samples of All-age Learning

Introduction   The ideas outlined in this section are simply samples, with the emphasis upon variety. It is hoped that the ideas provided will stimulate fuller and more appropriate plans to suit an individual community.

Significant people _____

Requirements   • Lined and plain paper, pencils and pens
     • An elderly, respected member of the community who is prepared to speak for a few minutes on 'How important Jesus is for me'

All those present are asked to take a piece of lined paper and, if they wish, a piece of plain paper, and go to a quiet corner of the room or hall. There they either write about or draw a picture of any person who has been important or significant in their lives. (The children may need assistance; they will, almost certainly, draw a picture of mum or dad, or both.) If they have time they could write a little prayer for their significant person. This should only take a maximum of five minutes.

All return together. Everyone is invited (no one is compelled) to show everyone else their picture and explain who it is and why that person is significant for them, or to read out what they have written.

When this has been completed the elderly member of the community explains simply 'How important Jesus is for me'. This short session can conclude with a time of prayer, reading aloud, for example, the prayers that have been written. The leader can bring the session to a conclusion with a prayer thanking God for Jesus; and a suitable hymn.

Which came first?_____

An opening question, sometimes asked by children – and secretly by not a few adults: *Which came first – dinosaurs or Adam and Eve?*

Requirements
- A good book from the local library (the children's section is the first and usually the best port of call) about the ages of the earth and the development of life on the planet.
- Three lengths of wallpaper (blank side to be used), about two metres long
- Pencils, colouring pens, glue, A4 white paper
- Three group leaders

Preparation
All the children and young people who are going to attend are invited to bring a model or toy 'dinosaur' with them and be ready, if they wish, to tell others about it. Adults are invited to bring their Bibles.

Divide those present into three mixed groups and give each its own working space or area. Each receives a length of wallpaper and a selection of writing and colouring pens.

The group leaders encourage the young people to show the group their dinosaurs and tell everyone what type it is and, if possible, when it roamed the planet. Each group then get to work on their own project.

- *Group 1* use the reference book on the ages of the earth and share out tasks. The wallpaper is divided lengthways into the principal ages from Precambrian to Holocene (including the Jurassic period and age of the dinosaurs). The young people locate where their dinosaurs fit in and each period is illustrated. Much adult help will be required. (Many adults will benefit from learning about dinosaurs from the youngsters.)

- *Group 2* read together the first story of creation in the Bible (Genesis 1:1-31 and 2:1-3). They then divide the length of wallpaper lengthways into seven sections representing the seven days. These are identified and illustrated according to what God created on each day. The seventh day could have a cartoon picture of 'God resting' (in a rocking chair perhaps!) or just the words 'The Sabbath, the Day of Rest', with pictures of the leisure or family things we do on Sundays.

- *Group 3* read together the second story of creation in the Bible (Genesis 2:4-25). The group will need to discuss how they are going to divide up their strip of wallpaper lengthways.

When the groups have their displays ready (or when time runs out) they gather together again and the three lengths are displayed, one above the other on an empty wall. The dinosaur sheet can go at the top, then the first story of the creation and under that the second story.

The session leader points out that there are two Bible accounts of creation, not just one, and they cannot both be accurate. In fact, they contradict one another. It can be seen, from the displays, that the accounts are quite different; they teach different messages, because that is what they are – teaching stories, rather like parables. The biblical stories of creation do not convey scientific fact, but religious teaching: that there is only one God, who is the mighty creator of all. The Bible stories do not set out to tell us the scientific *how*, but the religious *why* of creation. Other interesting lessons may be drawn, but care must be taken to do no more than answer the question, 'Which came first, dinosaurs or Adam and Eve?' Adults may like to continue the discussion another time.

Discipleship _____

Requirements

- An assortment of pens, pencils, colouring felt tips and crayons
- Plain A4 sheets of paper and rolls of redundant wallpaper

Divide into two groups, with the ages mixed. Everyone is told the theme and that each group will be given the name of one disciple of Jesus. They are to keep the name secret from the other group.

The groups separate to different rooms or areas, and prepare a presentation on their apostle – one group is given the name Simon Peter and the other Judas. Using the Bible and with the aid of a list of useful references, they may use any means they like – a collage, a poster, a play, for example – to show what sort of follower their named person was, with strengths and weaknesses, faults and failings.

Each group will be invited back to make a presentation to the other group. (Who goes first can be decided by the toss of a coin.) While accurate information must be given, the name of the disciple must not be used, because the other group will be timed to see how long it is before they accurately guess the correct name. To avoid random names being called out, there is a two-minute penalty on each inaccurate name suggested. (Naturally there has to be an agreed referee and score keeper.)

After each presentation has been made (and the presentation has to continue to its completion, even after the name has been discovered) – and a winner declared – with the aid of a blackboard, whiteboard or large sheet of paper, compare the two Apostles, like this:

Peter	*Judas*
Chosen by Jesus	Chosen by Jesus
Trusted by Jesus	Trusted by Jesus
Travelled with Jesus	Travelled with Jesus
Denied knowing Jesus	Betrayed Jesus
Ashamed of his action	Ashamed of his action
Hoped for forgiveness	Despaired of forgiveness
Told Jesus he loved him	Killed himself in despair

What lessons are there for each of us, no matter what age we are, as we try to be the followers of Jesus?

Moral tales _____

Requirements · A supply of paper and writing materials
· Several Ladybird books (see below)

With this activity adults must be reassured that although children's traditional stories are being used, there is a real value in being involved.

The number of stories used will depend upon the number of mixed groups of six people that can be made up, with different ages and genders. Each group needs one book. The Ladybird versions are standards in presentation and are very easily obtainable – most families have copies which they will be willing to loan. Use stories like *The Enormous Turnip, Chicken Licken, The Princess and the Frog, The Three Little Pigs, The Gingerbread Man, Beauty and the Beast*.

Each story has a clear moral. For example, *The Enormous Turnip* makes it clear that if all in a community, the greatest and the smallest, work together, even a huge task can be achieved. In *Chicken Licken* the moral is: do not blindingly follow a leader, without thought and question. (Very appropriate for teenagers who follow peers without question.)

The groups of six are given a book each (it is best not to let the groups choose) and sent off to their own venues, to read the story and work out the moral together. Each group then prepares its own dramatised version and thinks of a fresh way to convey the moral of the tale to the other groups. The group can also try to think of an incident in the life of Jesus, or one of his parables, which echoes or connects with the moral of the story.

There can be great fun when the plays are shared. With good leadership keeping it all together, it can be a very beneficial experience for all participants. Besides the content of the activity, shared events like this offer growth in a sense of community.

Get to know your Bible _____

Requirements

- Enough Bibles for one between two people. Booklets of questions are available from Gideons International (see page 111 for contact details). These have been supplied free of charge to schools and are excellent for all age groups to use.

The Bibles are distributed to pairs of people, where possible older more experienced church members with younger ones. A simple introduction is necessary along the lines of 'Let's now look at our Bibles and find where the Gospels are'.

Then the gathering split into pairs to work on the booklets. It might be a good idea to provide simple prizes, like bookmarks, for those who finish first, or in a given time.

Finding linked texts _____

Requirements
- Enough Bibles for one each, or one between two
- Lists of the following texts:

John 1:1	Matthew 26:26-28	Genesis 1:1
Ezekiel 34:11-13	2 Kings 1:7-8	Exodus 24:4-8
Mark 1:4-6	John 10:14-15	

Groups of four, as mixed as possible (young working with the more experienced), go off to a quiet area, equipped with the lists of texts. They are to look all the texts up and then pair them off. Then they decide what it is that promotes them to pair them up.

Before reassembling again each group must find two more pairs of texts for themselves. These they share with everyone else on return.

Bible characters: name bingo —

Requirements
- Two or three enthusiastic people who will spend time making the game, as instructed below

Preparation

This is a kind of name-bingo activity to involve all ages on the theme of 'People in the Bible'. Quite a lot of preparation is necessary for this game, but once it has been made it can be played again and again in the future.

1. Write a list of Old Testament names, at least 30. (The NIV Study Bible has a subject list which is invaluable.)
2. On an A5 sheet of paper, rule sixteen squares (four across, four down).
3. Randomly write three different names in three squares on line one, then repeat with other names for the remaining lines, making twelve names in total.
4. Repeat the last two steps on more sheets of paper (at least one for each person who will take part). Each sheet must be different.
5. Now make another set of names, and another set of papers divided into boxes, with New Testament names.
6. Copy all the names on to small cards, one name per card.

This is how the game is played:

1. Give each player a squared Old Testament and a New Testament sheet. Also give them 24 counters each. (Or you could photocopy the sheets, keeping the masters for use on another occasion, and use pencils to mark the squares.)
2. Place all the small cards face down. The caller picks up a card and calls out the name written on it.
3. Players with a square containing that name place a counter on it.
4. The first person to get a completed line – that is, three covered names – wins the first small prize. Then the game can continue for four lines or 'full house'.

Easter symbols _____

Requirements

- The 'symbols' listed below
- Separate areas where the groups can meet
- Writing, drawing and colouring materials for each group

The gathering is divided into six mixed-age groups, with no more than six to a group. If numbers dictate, repeat several of the groups, as necessary.

The session leader may give a short introduction outlining our need for symbols and signs, perhaps including a comment that Easter bunnies occupy no place in Christian symbolism!

The groups are directed to separate areas and on arrival each is given an Easter symbol – a picture or, if possible, the real thing.

- *Group 1* receives an Easter or Paschal candle (it can be a used one from a previous year).
- *Group 2* is loaned an Easter egg.
- *Group 3* is given a hot-cross bun.
- *Group 4* receives a picture of a lamb (or a cuddly knitted one).
- *Group 5* is given a picture of an empty tomb.
- *Group 6* gets a picture of a butterfly.

The groups are told to discuss the meaning of their symbol. The adults agree upon the wording of a written presentation (including as much historical and biblical background information as they can gather) while the youngsters can prepare a poster showing the symbol (which will be left behind in the group area when the group returns to the general gathering) with a few accompanying words.

After 20 to 30 minutes, the groups re-assemble, and then in turn make a presentation of their poster and their written work. Care must be taken to involve the younger members in this part of the activity.

The Easter walk

Requirements • None

This can be used as part of any Easter-time learning activity. Based on the story in Luke 24:13-35, the action recital is fun for all ages. All should stand, with the leader in full view.

The leader reads the words below and everyone repeats them	*At the same time the leader shows the action, which all copy.*
Two friends of Jesus were walking to Emmaus.	*holds up index finger of each hand*
They were talking to one another	*talking gesture with left hand*
about all that had happened.	*move right arm from side to side*
While they were talking	*talking gesture with left hand*
Jesus joined them,	*walk on spot*
but they did not recognise him.	*shake head*
Jesus said to them,	*talking gesture with hand*
'What are you talking about?'	*hold palms outstretched and half-extended*
They told of Jesus' death on the cross	*make a cross with two fingers*
and how three days later	*hold up three fingers*
women found the tomb empty.	*shrug shoulders*
Jesus said to the two,	*talking gesture*
'How slow you are to believe	*hand on heart*

what the scriptures say.'	*open hand like a book*
The disciples asked Jesus to stay	*summoning action with hand*
and eat with them.	*action of eating*
At supper Jesus took the bread,	*hold out right hand*
blessed it and broke it.	*two hands break bread*
Then they recognised him,	*take hands away from eyes*
but Jesus had disappeared.	*look around*
The disciples hurried back to Jerusalem	*walk quickly on spot*
and told the apostles	*talking gesture*
all they had seen.	*right finger points to eyes*
How they recognised Jesus	*take hands away from eyes*
at the breaking of the bread.	*two hands break bread*

An Easter trial _____

This could take place at any time of the year.

Requirements
- A large room or hall set out to suggest a courtroom – for example, a judge's raised chair (perhaps borrowed from the church); two rows of benches for the jury; a 'boxed' area for the witness stand
- Volunteers to take the key parts; others to be members of the jury, who only have to listen and vote. (If there are too many for the jury, then there can be a public gallery; if too few, spread the number over the jury benches.)

Preparation
Those portraying the characters of Mary Magdalene, Simon Peter, John, Mary, mother of James, Salome, the guards, Mark the evangelist (who is in the dock), etc., are given several days to read Mark 15:33-47 and 16:1-20. They have to think themselves into the part and read between the lines of the Gospel, so as to present a rounded character in court.

A 'distinguished' judge is required and clerks of the court. Parts must be found for the young people – for example, Salome can be a young girl, and some of the boys can be the guards.

John Mark is in the dock and there is a prosecutor who calls witnesses to attest, on oath, that they really did find the tomb empty, for instance.

Before the trial begins everyone must be told that all actors can develop their character's story as much as they wish, as long as they do not deviate from the basic story, as told by Mark.

The charge before the court, read by the clerk of the court, is: 'That the accused, John Mark, formerly a resident of Jerusalem, has deceived the Human Race by his fraudulent account that the tomb of Jesus of Nazareth, a convicted criminal, was empty and that Jesus appeared alive to a group of his friends.'

The judge needs to have a thorough understanding of the Gospel text and gently give directions to the court, if necessary.

If time permits, it is worthwhile to conclude with a review session.

The meaning of love _____

Requirements
- Large sheets of white paper (one for each of the groups to make a poster)
- Large felt-tipped colouring pens
- Six areas for the groups to work in (the groups are numbered one to six)

The gathering is divided into six equal groups of adults and young people. A large sheet of paper for a poster and colouring pens are given to each group, and each has an appointed leader.

The groups go to their areas and only then are they told that each has a letter: Group 1 – **C**, 2 – **A**, 3– **R**, 4 – **I**, 5 – **N**, 6 – **G.** This letter is to be drawn, as large as possible, on one side of the sheet paper. (The group should keep its letter secret from the other groups.)

The group leader now leads a short discussion on 'What is love?' The young people's ideas should be taken note of, as well as the adults'. After about five minutes the leader tells the group that they have to think up a completion to the caption, 'Love is. . .'. After talking it over, the group may decide on something like 'Love is putting others first' or 'Love is belonging to a family'. The group should talk it through and together agree on the caption and the illustration. The group should not blindly accept the first suggestion proposed.

The completed caption is now copied on to the blank side of the sheet of paper. The caption can then be decorated. The leader must ensure that this is a group activity involving all ages.

The completed poster is kept a secret from the other groups. One of the group (not the leader) is deputed to show the poster off at the appropriate time.

All groups are recalled and the leader calls out the poster-bearers to sit or stand in line in numerical order from left to right, so that, when held up to view, at the direction of the leader, the hidden word CARING is spelt out. When reversed each poster shows the 'Love is . . .' side to the whole gathering and the poster-bearer reads out the caption. Each remains standing while the leader says *a few* words about the love that Jesus asks from us all. Not a romantic love, or even a friendship love, but a caring and respecting love, which should embrace everyone. Paul's description of love in 1 Corinthians 13:4-7 could be read here, or 1 John 4:7-21. Then at a signal all the posters are turned round again to reveal the word CARING.

Capernaum _____

Requirements
- Sufficient copies of Peter's house (see below) for each group to have two or three each. Young artists may be encouraged, some days before, to copy the picture and have it enlarged on a photocopier.
- Maps of Israel, one for each group. The Israeli Tourist Board, with an office in London, or a tour operator that arranges for groups to go to the Holy Land, will be happy to supply copies.

Opening note
Jesus was born in Bethlehem and brought up in Nazareth, but at the opening of his ministry he was driven out of his home town and made Capernaum his new home and the centre of his ministry. At the site of that lakeside town modern archaeologists have identified and excavated the family home of Peter, where Jesus is believed to have lived with the family. The artist's impression below is based upon the discoveries at the site; it is as authentic a picture of the excavated house as can be achieved. (The house stands only some fifty yards from the lakeside.)

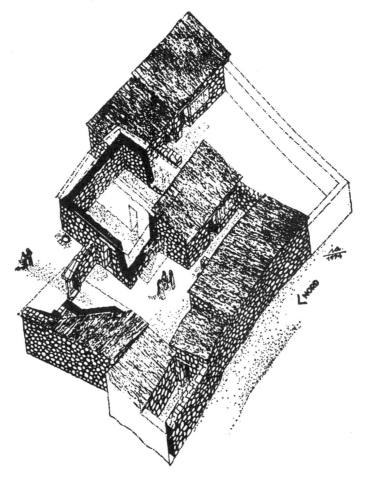

When assembled, the gathering needs to be divided into all-age groups of six to eight people. These groups, in turn, are divided into two: the older members and the younger. A picture of the house is given to each sub-group to work on separately.

The older group is asked to look at the picture and decide which part of the house would have housed Peter and his wife and family; which would have been the part lived in by Peter's mother-in-law; which room would possibly have been used by Jesus; and what the remaining rooms, areas and spaces would have been used for.

After discussion and mutual agreement, the picture can be marked, and on the reverse reasons given for the choice. Next, using the map of Israel, the sub-group must decide why Jesus chose to live in this particular town, listing the advantages and disadvantages from the point of view of his ministry.

Meanwhile, the young people (provided they are old enough) separately answer the same questions.

After sufficient time each group re-assembles and the two sub-sections of each group compare notes. When some measure of common agreement is reached, the group is ready to report back to the general gathering.

'North' meets 'South'

Requirements
- Two large separate rooms or halls and two leaders who have been prepared
- A 'scribe' for each group with writing materials
- Two free-standing whiteboards for the presentation

Divide the gathering into two groups of equal size, with equal distribution of ages in each. One is the 'North' and the other is the 'South' – for the purpose of this demonstration, the 'South' implies all the developing (Third World) countries and the 'North' western Europe, North America and Australia.

The two groups are situated in two separate places so that neither can see what the other is preparing. Each group will need a leader and a scribe to record and report back.

The 'North' group is told that all the members live in Britain, another western European country, North America or Australia. (This information should only be given when the group has separated from the 'South'.) They are to make a comprehensive list of the electrical goods that each family has – colour televisions, stereo units, computers, dishwashers and so on. (Include the number where there are several of one item in a household.) The leader of this group can encourage the subtle competitive spirit which will become evident: 'We have four TVs'; 'Well, we've got one in every room'. The children and young people must be involved and each encouraged to complete the statement, 'I could not live without . . .'. (Answers are likely to include the TV and stereo unit.)

The 'South' group is told that their members live in Asia, Africa, South America or any developing (Third World) country in the Southern Hemisphere. They are to make a list of the possessions they are likely to have – a hut, a bowl, a spoon, one change of clothes, for example. The children and young people are encouraged to pretend that they live in such a society and complete the statement, 'I could not live without . . .'.

When the two groups are reunited, after fifteen minutes or so, the 'North' are invited to present their findings first (the impact is lost if the 'South' go first). If possible, the presentation should be graphic and visual, listing items and numbers on a black- or whiteboard. (Each group might bring its freestanding whiteboard with it and stand them side by side.)

The second group then makes its presentation on the other board, pointing out that the people of the 'South' have no electrical supply or water in their homes.

The conclusion will be self-evident. We who live in western Europe are very rich compared to those who live in the developing countries.

This activity can be followed by

- a service which reminds those present of Christ's warning to the rich (Matthew 19:16-26 and 25:31-46);
- a further activity to explore why there is such a huge gap between rich and poor;
- plans to twin with a poor community abroad
- plans to raise funds for Christian Aid, CAFOD, etc.

Other ideas can be found in the excellent *It's Not Fair: A Handbook on World Development for Youth Groups* (Christian Aid / CAFOD).

The colourful world of the New Testament _____

This activity is suitable for a full day event.

Requirements
- Library books
- Craft materials (see below)

Preparation

The Bible was written in a culture and land vastly different from our own. It is essential, therefore, that we understand the life-styles, manners and customs of that time if we are going to fully understand scripture. The following can be adapted to the time available, filling an hour, or, more usefully, a half or whole day. The more time given to it, the more the whole community will benefit, because the aim would be to mount an exhibition afterwards in the church, for all to see and learn from.

In preparation a member of the planning team should visit the local library (central or main branch) and explain the project. Most libraries run a topic book loan scheme, whereby they will collect together for you a whole range of books on the subject, suitable for all ages. (There are many excellent books currently available, including those published by Lion, Usborne and Dorling Kindersley.)

The all-age gathering needs to be divided into three equal groups. They will be the 'Romans', the 'Greeks' and the 'Jews'. In the opening session the leader points out that Jesus lived in a society that was influenced by three cultures – Greek, Roman and Aramaic (or Jewish). Jesus would have spoken some Greek, Hebrew and Aramaic; the Romans occupied this country and Greek amphitheatres and culture were everywhere.

Each group leader will need a little preparation before the day, in conjunction with the other two, to discuss and agree the topics to be explored. These should include, for example, housing, food, religion. Each group is sent away to explore the same topics, using the books provided for their research. The children and young people can be fully employed, copying pictures from the books, making artefacts in clay, card, leather, and so on.

It can be a very exciting and most productive day for all involved. Time should be allowed for each group to show off their achievements to the other two, and to mount the display for the church.

Living a community life _____

This is a suggestion for a full-day activity. It is advisable to produce a programme well before the event so that people, especially busy parents, can make plans to attend. The timetable should be followed strictly, and even if events do not flow as intended for the day, the lunch break and the departure time should be adhered to. People will not support further days if they cannot rely upon the times advertised.

Aim

It is important to have a clear purpose for an event which involves a whole or a part of a day. The objective for this event is twofold: to help all participants to have a better insight, according to their degree of maturity, into the life of religious sisters; and to appreciate that a relevant form of worship is at the centre of every Christian community.

Requirements

- The video *Sister Act*, with permission to use it, if necessary, and equipment
- A leader for the day who has already watched the video and made appropriate notes, bearing in mind the aim of the day. From the list of participants who have enrolled for the day make up two equal-sized, mixed groups. (If there are fewer than sixteen, adapt the programme for one group.)
- A religious sister, either Roman Catholic or Anglican, as a guest speaker. (Seek the advice of a local Catholic or Anglican priest.)

The idea of the day is to show everyone the video *Sister Act*, then explore in two separate groups the questions:

- Does the film realistically show religious life as lived today?
- Could the worship of our own community be enlivened?

Programme for the day

10am	Welcome and introduction
10.10am	Watch the video together
11.40am	*Break for refreshments*
11.50am	Group work A
12.30pm	*Lunch break*
1.30pm	Group work B
2.10pm	General assembly: question time

2.45pm	Prepare for Act of Worship
3.15pm	Act of Worship
3.45pm	Appraisal sheets completed
4pm	*Departure*

Notes During the Welcome and Introduction the leader should very simply explain what the day will cover and explore. The guest speaker should be introduced and everyone invited to talk to her during the breaks.

Fruits of the Spirit _____

Requirements
- Nine different 'fruits' – for example, apple, pear, banana, orange, kiwifruit, strawberry, grapes, lychee, lemon
- Nine sheets of white A4 paper for each group

The assembly is divided into mixed age groups of five or six people (no more than nine groups) and provided with an area to work in. A table and chairs for each group would make life easier.

Each group is given at least one of the fruits, nine pieces of plain paper and the text from Galatians 5:22-23 on the fruits of the Spirit. This exercise is intended to be fun and not taken too seriously.

The leader asks the groups to go away and decide which of the 'fruits' of the Spirit – love, joy, peace, etc. – they think is represented by the fruit they have been given. When the groups have discussed and decided on their reply – with reasons for their choice – they go on to write the nine fruits of the Spirit on the sheets provided and draw the fruit which they believe best illustrates that quality of the Spirit.

After 20-30 minutes each group reports back with their pictures – and reasons for their choices.

Celebrating freedom

This is a proposal for a full or half-day activity. (It could be used for young people alone, as part of a confirmation programme.) It is advisable to produce a programme well before the event so that participants, particularly busy parents, can make plans to attend. The timetable should, as far as possible, be followed strictly and even if events do not flow as intended for the day, the lunch break and the departure time should be firmly adhered to. People will not support further events if they cannot rely upon the times that are advertised.

Aim

The aim and purpose must be clear in the organiser's/leader's mind; otherwise the direction and purpose of the event will be lost. The desired outcomes for this event are:

- a deepened understanding and appreciation of freedom in general
- a better knowledge and understanding of the work of Christ, in winning us freedom from sin
- a better understanding and realisation that films and television programmes can challenge us to think more deeply and show us that religious themes are relevant to life

Requirements

- A leader for the day who has already seen, and thought about, *Chicken Run*
- A copy of the video and equipment to show it
- Bibles

Preparation

The leader should watch the video in advance of the day and make notes, bearing in mind the aim of the event. From the list of participants, make up five mixed age groups. They will be called *Fowler, Babs, Rocky, Ginger* and *Mac* (Five of the characters in *Chicken Run*.) Each group needs an area to work in and a Bible.

The idea of the day is for everyone to watch the video *Chicken Run* and then go into their groups to discuss their character, making a list of his/her strengths and weaknesses and what part they play in the story. When the groups gather together, the leader traces briefly the story of the chickens' struggle to be free. Each group leader then shares the insights of the group on their character. The next task for each group is to return to their areas, with the Bible, to find one Old Testament and one New Testament story that parallels the story of *Chicken Run*. Groups report back and then the leader leads a discussion on how Christ won freedom for us from the slavery of sin.

Possible programme for the day

10am	Welcome and introductions
10.10am	Watch the video together
11.40am	*Break for refreshments*
11.50am	Group work: exploring our character
12.30pm	*Lunch break*
1.15pm	Groups report back
1.40pm	Group work with Bibles
2.10pm	General assembly: sharing and discussion
2.45pm	Prepare for Act of Worship
3.15pm	Act of Worship
3.45pm	Review of the event – publicly or with review sheets

Act of Worship

The aim is to thank God in appreciation of our *freedom from* injustice and hunger, for example, in our country, and *freedom to* pursue and practise our own religious faith, choice of career, and so on; and to intercede for those who do not enjoy these basic freedoms.

Use should be made of the scripture texts used during the day, with appropriate songs and hymns. Recorded music, perhaps suggested by the young people, could play an important part.

APPENDIX

Addresses St Paul Multimedia Productions
Middle Green
Slough
SL1 6BS

Telephone 01753 577629
Fax 01753 511809

Turvey Abbey
Turvey
MK43 8DE

Telephone 01234 881432

Gideons International
Western House
George Street
Lutterworth
Leicestershire
LE17 4EE

Telephone 01455 554241
Fax 01455 558267

How to make playdough 1 cup plain flour

Half a cup salt

2 tablespoons oil

2 teaspoons cream of tartar

1 cup water with food colouring added

Place all the ingredients in a non-stick saucepan and mix with a wooden spoon. Cook on a medium to high heat, stirring all the time until the mixture comes together in a lump. Keep in an airtight container or plastic bag.